The Glasgow Novel
a complete guide

Third edition

Moira Burgess

The Scottish Library Association
Glasgow City Council Cultural and Leisure Services
1999

The Scottish Library Association
Scottish Centre for Information & Library Services
1 John Streeet
Hamilton ML3 7EU

 Glasgow City Council Cultural and Leisure Services
The Mitchell Library
North Street
Glasgow G3 7DN

The publishers acknowledge subsidy from the Scottish Arts Council towards the publication of this volume

Design & layout Margaret Thomson, Graphics Department, Mitchell Library
Cover photograph Trinity Towers by Alan Wright

ISBN 0 900649 42 9

Printed by Cordfall Ltd. Glasgow

Contents

Illustrations

Every effort has been made to seek the permission of copyright holders to reproduce photographs used in this publication

Foreword

The first edition of this bibliography was published in 1972 by the Scottish Library Association, having originated as part of a thesis on the Glasgow novel 1870-1970, submitted in 1971 for the degree of Master of Arts in the University of Strathclyde. While the first edition observed the same chronological boundaries as the thesis, this limitation was removed in the second edition published in 1986. The third edition similarly contains, it is hoped, all novels about Glasgow however early their setting or publication date, and includes all Glasgow novels (and collections of short stories) published to the end of 1997.

The scope of the bibliography, apart from the extension of its time zone, remains as stated in the introduction to the first edition:

> 'The Glasgow novel'… has been taken to imply a novel which is set wholly or substantially in Glasgow (or in a quasi-fictional city readily recognisable as Glasgow) or which, though perhaps containing only a short Glasgow section, conveys a genuine picture of the life, character or atmosphere of the city. Hence it is not necessarily (though in practice it is very often) written by a Glasgow author; conversely, books by Glasgow authors not set in the city are not included.

As before, the geographical zone covered is, roughly, 'Glasgow as it officially exists today', though in 1972 we evidently did not foresee the series of boundary changes consequent on two local government reorganisations. To inhabitants on the outskirts who think their area should, or should not, be included, we can only promise a future rethinking when official Glasgow seems to have taken a final shape.

As before, too, 'much of the material included is not of high literary quality'. Over the years we have become a little more hospitable to the light detective story, which the first edition did not include. In the case of long series of thrillers, such as those by Knox and Malloch, we have generally listed one title as an example, referring the reader for the full canon to Hamish Whyte's bibliography of Glasgow crime fiction, cited in the reading list.

Two other recent developments have augmented the number of Glasgow novels without much gain to literature: the choice of Glasgow as a background for popular romantic sagas, quite often in the form of trilogies or quartets, and an explosion of self-publishing. We have done our best to keep pace with the results.

The survey of the Glasgow novel, based on the text of the original thesis and first included in the second edition, has been updated and improved. Space has not permitted more than an introduction to the subject, but the interested reader may perhaps proceed to the further suggestions in the reading list. This has been considerably expanded, since criticism of Glasgow fiction, both in general and in relation to individual authors, has greatly increased in recent years. We have deleted a few entries which appeared in the second edition, generally because they have been supplanted by recent writing.

Certain shorthand terms have again been used in the annotations to denote groups or schools among Glasgow novels: *urban kailyard* (the lace-curtain view of city life); *industrial* or *proletarian* novels, flourishing particularly in the 'thirties; the *gangland* novel, school of *No mean city*; and the *realistic* novel, 'which attempts… to set down Glasgow life as it is'. The appearance, since the first edition, of many novels which refuse to fit neatly into any of these categories – Friel's *Mr Alfred M.A.*, Gray's *Lanark*, Kuppner's *A very quiet street*, Kennedy's *So I am glad*, and more – is a very healthy sign for the Glasgow novel.

Most of the research for this bibliography has been done in The Mitchell Library, Glasgow, and particular thanks are due to the staffs of the History and Glasgow and Arts departments there. I am also indebted, however, to all those friends and acquaintances who have brought to my attention many titles which I might have missed, and many, indeed, which I did miss when preparing earlier editions. Thanks to their efforts, this edition, while not claiming perfection, is certainly more comprehensive than either of its predecessors, and, it is hoped, will be correspondingly more useful to the student, critic or interested reader of Glasgow novels.

Reading List

1 Bibliographies

LECLAIRE, LUCIEN. *A general analytical bibliography of the regional novelists of the British Isles, 1800-1950.* Paris: Societe d'Edition 'Les Belles Lettres', 1954.

WHYTE, HAMISH. *Glasgow crime fiction: a bibliographical guide.* Glasgow: The Mitchell Library, 1977. Aimed to fill the gap left by Burgess: *The Glasgow novel* (1972), which excluded the light detective story. Available in typescript at The Mitchell Library, Glasgow. New edition in preparation.

MORGAN, EDWIN. *Twentieth century Scottish classics.* Glasgow: Book Trust Scotland, 1987. Includes some 20 Glasgow novels.

BURGESS, MOIRA. *Glasgow books and writers of the twentieth century.* Glasgow: Book Trust Scotland, 1990. A select bibliography with brief biographical notes for each writer; includes novelists, poets and playwrights.

GLASGOW CITY LIBRARIES AND ARCHIVES. *Imagining a city: 20th century Glasgow writing*; compiled by Hamish Whyte. Glasgow: City Libraries and Archives, 1997. Catalogue of a thematic exhibition in The Mitchell Library; selected titles (fiction, poetry and drama). Includes an overview of twentieth-century Glasgow literature by Moira Burgess.

2 Unpublished Sources

Manuscripts of many Glasgow novelists are held in the National Library of Scotland, Edinburgh, and The Mitchell Library, Glasgow, whose catalogues should be consulted.

BURGESS, MOIRA. 'The Glasgow novel 1870-1970: a survey and bibliography.' M.A. thesis, University of Strathclyde, 1971. The original thesis on which the present bibliography is based.

James Barke Papers. In The Mitchell Library, Glasgow. Several boxes of correspondence, mss, personal and family documents.

CAMERON, IAIN. 'George Friel: an introduction to his life and work.' M.Litt. thesis, University of Edinburgh, 1987.

Fifty letters from George Mills to George Cruickshank, 1848-75. In The Mitchell Library, Glasgow. Includes references to the writing and publishing history of *The beggar's benison.*

Eleven letters of R.B. Cunninghame Graham to Frederick Niven: with a letter to Mr John Dunlop… from Mrs Frederick Niven. In The Mitchell Library, Glasgow.

3 General: Literary History and Criticism

BROWN, D. WALKER. *Clydeside litterateurs: biographical sketches.* Glasgow: Carter and Pratt, 1897. Brief notes (with portrait drawings and facsimile autographs) of 39 contemporary writers born in or connected with Glasgow.

KILPATRICK, JAMES A. *Literary landmarks of Glasgow*. Glasgow: St Mungo Press, 1898. Anecdotal but useful literary history of Glasgow from the seventeenth century on.

EYRE-TODD, GEORGE. *The Glasgow poets*. Glasgow: William Hodge, 1903. Biographies and poems. A number of the poets are also fiction writers.

STEWART, AGNES. 'Some Scottish novelists.' *The Northern Review*, vol. 1, no. 1, May 1924, p. 35-41. Mentions several Glasgow novelists.

GRIEVE, C. M. *Contemporary Scottish studies: first series*. Leonard Parsons, 1926. See chapter 10, 'Frederick Niven: J. J. Bell' and chapters 38 and 39, 'Newer Scottish fiction'.

LOCHHEAD, MARION C. 'The Glasgow school.' *Scots Magazine*, vol. 4, no. 4, January 1926, p. 277-81. Notes on contemporary Glasgow novelists; remarks on the potential material for 'the great Glasgow book'.

MACDONALD, ANGUS. 'Modern Scots novelists.' *Edinburgh essays on Scots literature*. Edinburgh: Oliver and Boyd, 1933. Includes 'the Glasgow school'.

COCKBURN, JOHN. 'The Scottish novel: can we uphold a renaissance that lacks the thing that matters?' *Scots Observer*, 25 February 1933, p. 9. Sees the lack of a good industrial novel as 'a glaring weakness in the field of realistic fiction'.

SCOULLER, EDWARD D. 'My view of the Scots novel.' *Scotland*, vol. 3, no. 4, Winter 1938, p. 49-52. Considers the 'new school' of realistic novelists.

GUNN. NEIL M. 'Drains for the kraal.' *Glasgow Herald*, 4 January 1941, p. 3. On the need for working-class fiction written 'from the inside'.

BLAKE, GEORGE. *Barrie and the Kailyard school*. Arthur Barker, 1951. Chiefly on the Kailyarders, but comments also on the lack of industrial fiction and suggests reasons.

BLAKE, GEORGE. *Annals of Scotland 1895-1955: an essay on the twentieth-century Scottish novel*. British Broadcasting Corporation, [1956]. Accompanied a series of radio adaptations broadcast 1956-57. Notes the rise of the 'proletarian' novel from the 1930s onwards.

BLAKE, GEORGE. 'Belles lettres and boaters.' *Glasgow Herald*, 16 November 1957. The journalistic and literary scene in 1920s Glasgow; reminiscences of, among others, Neil Munro and J. J. Bell.

MACK, J.A. 'The changing city.' *Third statistical account of Scotland: Glasgow*, edited J. Cunnison and J. B. S. Gilfillan. Glasgow: Collins, 1958. Considers novels and sketches as source material for social history.

MITCHELL, JACK. 'The struggle for the working-class novel in Scotland.' *Scottish Marxist*, no. 6, April 1974, p. 40-52; no. 7, October 1974, p. 46-54; no. 8, January 1975, p. 39-48. Extracted from a long article in *Zeitschrift fur Anglistik und Amerikanistik*, 21(4), [1973].

GIFFORD, DOUGLAS. 'Scottish fiction since 1945.' *Scottish writing and writers*, edited Norman Wilson. Edinburgh: Ramsay Head Press, 1977. Wide-ranging survey including many Glasgow writers, and considering at some length 'the tradition of *No mean city*, in which the writer turns his attention to the obvious blight of city life in Glasgow and the big cities'.

HUNTER, STEWART. 'A reader's regrets.' *Scots Magazine*, new series, vol. 106, no. 4, January

1977, p. 369-75. A personal survey of Scottish fiction in the 1920s and 1930s.

HART, FRANCIS RUSSELL. *The Scottish novel: a critical survey*. John Murray, 1978.

McCABE, BRIAN. 'No real city.' *New Edinburgh Review*, no. 54, May 1981, p. 10-12. On Glasgow fiction: an early recognition of the importance of Alasdair Gray's *Lanark*.

ELLIOT, ROBERT. 'Women, Glasgow, and the novel.' *Chapman* 33, vol. 7, no. 3, Autumn 1982, p. 1-4. Discusses the small number and (allegedly) 'undistinguished' output of Glasgow women novelists, and suggests possible reasons.

MACAFEE, CAROLINE. 'Glasgow dialect in literature.' *Scottish Language*, no. 1, Autumn 1982, p. 45-53. Includes consideration of dialect as used by Kelman, Alex Hamilton and McIlvanney.

THOMSON, GEDDES. 'The Glasgow short story.' *Chapman* 33, vol. 7, no. 3, Autumn 1982, p. 5-8.

MACAFEE, CAROLINE. *Glasgow.* Amsterdam/Philadelphia: John Benjamins, 1983. 'Not just a synopsis of Glasgow English through texts with linguistic commentary but a conspectus of Glasgow's social and economic history and of the present-day socio-economic background...' Considers a number of texts by Glasgow novelists.

MORGAN, EDWIN. 'Glasgow speech in recent Scottish literature.' *Scotland and the lowland tongue*, edited J. D. McClure. Aberdeen: University Press, 1983. (Reprinted in Edwin Morgan, *Crossing the border: essays on Scottish literature*, 1990.)

GIFFORD, DOUGLAS. *The dear green place? The novel in Glasgow and Strathclyde*. Glasgow: Third Eye Centre, 1985. Essay examining the portrayal of Glasgow in fiction during the twentieth century.

NOBLE, ANDREW. 'Urbane silence: Scottish writing and the nineteenth-century city.' *Perspectives of the Scottish city*, edited George Gordon. Aberdeen: University Press, 1985. Comments on the perceived lack of 'city novels' in Scottish Victorian literature.

DONALDSON, WILLIAM. *Popular literature in Victorian Scotland: language, fiction and the press*. Aberdeen: University Press, 1986. Shows that 'city novels' were being written, often for serial publication. See especially chapter 3 on David Pae. See also Donaldson's *The language of the people: Scots prose from the Victorian revival* (AUP 1989), an anthology of vernacular pieces published in Scottish newspapers and journals 1855-1905, including a number from Glasgow.

BERRY, SIMON and WHYTE, HAMISH eds. *Glasgow observed.* Edinburgh: John Donald, 1987. Anthology of prose extracts 'illuminating 200 years of Glasgow history'; includes passages from several Glasgow novels.

MALZAHN, MANFRED. 'The industrial novel.' *The history of Scottish literature, vol. 4: Twentieth century*, edited Cairns Craig. Aberdeen: University Press, 1987; chapter 15.

HOBSBAUM, PHILIP. 'The Glasgow group.' *Edinburgh Review* 80-81, May 1988, p. 59-63. Describes his involvement with two Glasgow writing groups, whose members included Kelman, Liz Lochhead, Gray and Tom Leonard.

BURGESS, MOIRA. 'The novelist's map of Glasgow.' *A Glasgow collection*, edited Kevin McCarra and Hamish Whyte. Glasgow: City Libraries, 1990, p. 13-23. Considers options for the treatment of Glasgow place-names in fiction writing.

McKEAN, CHARLES. 'Architecture and the Glasgows of the imagination.' *A Glasgow collection, op.cit.,* p. 99-106. Glasgow architecture as 'an historical anchor [to the] chymerical… Glasgows of the mind'.

MALZAHN, MANFRED. 'Coming to terms with industrial Scotland: two "proletarian" novels of the 1930s.' *Studies in Scottish fiction: twentieth century, 1900-1950,* edited Joachim Schwend and Horst Drescher. Frankfurt: Peter Lang, 1990, p. 193-205. On Blake's *The shipbuilders* and Barke's *Major operation.*

SPRING, IAN. *Phantom village: the myth of the new Glasgow.* Edinburgh: Polygon, 1990. Considers the mythology and truth of Glasgow as presented in various media. One chapter (p. 92-102) devoted to *Lanark.*

WHYTE, CHRISTOPHER. 'Imagining the city: the Glasgow novel.' *Studies in Scottish fiction: twentieth century, 1900-1950, op. cit.,* p. 317-33.

PORTER, DOROTHY. 'Imagining a city.' *Chapman* 63, January 1991, p. 42-50.

MORGAN, EDWIN. 'Tradition and experiment in the Glasgow novel.' *The Scottish novel since the seventies: new visions, old dreams,* edited Gavin Wallace and Randall Stevenson. Edinburgh: University Press, 1993, p. 85-98.

BURGESS, MOIRA. *Reading Glasgow: a… literary guide to authors and books associated with the city.* Edinburgh: Book Trust Scotland, 1996. Takes a 'guidebook' approach, describing 'first what traces of [Glasgow writers] remain, and then what traces of the city can be found in their work'.

BURGESS, MOIRA. 'The Glasgow short story.' *Laverock,* [2, October 1996], p. 18-22.

HARVIE, DAVID. *Lines around the city.* Glasgow: Lindsay Publications, 1997. Anthology structured on the fifteen stations of the Glasgow Underground system, with fiction, poetry and non-fiction extracts relating to each area.

BURGESS, MOIRA. *Imagine a city: Glasgow in fiction.* Glendaruel: Argyll Publishing, 1998. A critical history of Glasgow fiction from the eighteenth century to date.

4   Individual Authors: Biography and Criticism
Allan, Dot
KYLE, ELISABETH. 'Dot Allan.' *Scots Observer,* 25 June 1931, p. 4.
Banks, Iain
McGILLIVRAY, ALAN. 'The worlds of Iain Banks.' *Laverock,* [2, October 1996], p. 22-27. Includes *Espedair Street* and *The crow road.*
Barke, James
James Barke Papers: see 'Unpublished sources' above.
SCOULLER, EDWARD. 'So this is Glasgow!' *Outlook,* vol. 1, no. 8, November 1936, p. 79-81. Long review of *Major operation.*
BARKE, JAMES. *The green hills far away: a chapter in autobiography.* Collins, 1940. On 'the Tulliallan years', 1907-18; cf fictional treatment in *The land of the leal.*

MITCHELL, JACK. 'James Barke.' Scottish Marxist, no. 8, January 1975, p. 39-48. Part of 'The struggle for the working-class novel in Scotland', *op.cit.*

Bell, J. J.

GRIEVE, C. M. 'Frederick Niven: J. J. Bell.' Chapter 10 in his *Contemporary Scottish studies* (1926), op.cit.

'The man you know: no. 93a.' *Glasgow Weekly Herald,* 23 December 1933.

BELL, J. J. *I remember.* Edinburgh: Porpoise Press, 1932. Memoirs of the 1870s and 1880s in Glasgow, with some autobiographical content. Also *Do you remember?* (1934).

BELL, J. J. 'Introduction: the story of the book.' *Wee Macgreegor*, new library edition. Edinburgh: Moray Press, 1933. Origins and publishing history of *Wee Macgreegor*.

Black, William

'Men you know – no. 226'. *The Bailie*, no. 226, 14 February 1877, p. 1-2.

REID, [THOMAS] WEMYSS. *William Black: novelist.* Cassell, 1902. See p. 26-33 on *James Merle.*

Blake, George

BLAKE, GEORGE. *Vagabond papers.* Glasgow: Walter Wilson and Co., 1922. 24 newspaper essays: see I, 'A woman of destiny', possibly the genesis of *Mince Collop Close.*

HUNTER, STEWART. 'George Blake's Firth of Clyde.' *Scots Magazine,* vol. 66, no. 1, October 1956, p. 52-58. Suggests locations for Blake's fictional place-names, mainly in his 'Garvel' (Greenock) novels.

REID, ALEXANDER. 'Ends and means: a study of George Blake.' *Scotland's Magazine,* vol. 55, no. 11, November 1959, p. 37-38.

HUNTER, STEWART. 'Waters of change.' *Scots Magazine,* vol. 94, no. 4, January 1971, p. 322-30. Compares Blake's treatment of depression years in *The shipbuilders* with the writer's memories of the same period.

McCLEERY, ALISON and ALISTAIR. 'Personality of place in the urban regional novel.' *Scottish Geographical Magazine,* vol. 97, no. 2, September 1981, p. 66-77. On *The shipbuilders.*

Boyd, Edward

ROSS, RAYMOND J. 'The view from Eddie Boyd.' *Cencrastus,* no. 27, Autumn 1987, p. 4-6. Interview with Eddie Boyd. Followed (p. 6-9) by 'Across the airwaves', an edited version of a BBC Radio programme on Boyd which was never broadcast.

BOYD, EDWARD. 'Green water without grace.' *Cencrastus,* no. 39, Spring 1991, p. 3-11; no. 40, Summer 1991, p. 30-35.

Carswell, Catherine

CARSWELL, CATHERINE. *The savage pilgrimage.* Chatto and Windus, 1932. Biography of D. H. Lawrence; describes his influence and encouragement in the writing of *Open the door!*

CARSWELL, CATHERINE. *Lying awake: an unfinished autobiography.* Secker and Warburg, 1950.

CARSWELL, JOHN. 'Introduction'. *Open the door!,* Virago edition 1986, p. v-xvii.

Biographical notes by Carswell's son. See also the Introduction by Ianthe Carswell to *The camomile*, Virago edition 1987, p. vii-xv.

SMALL, CHRISTOPHER. 'Catherine Carswell: engagement and detachment.' *Chapman* 74-75, Autumn/Winter 1993, p. 131-36. See also Margaret Elphinstone, 'Four pioneering novels', p. 23-39, which deals with *Open the door!*

McCULLOCH, MARGERY PALMER. 'Opening the door: women, Carswell and the Scottish Renaissance.' *Scottish Studies/Etudes Ecossaises: Proceedings of the Scottish workshop of the ESSE conference, Bordeaux 1993.* Grenoble: Université Stendhal and Germersheim: Johannes Gutenberg Universität Mainz, 1994, p. 93-104.

PILDITCH, JAN. 'Opening the door on Catherine Carswell.' *Scotlands,* 2/1994, 1995, p. 53-65.

SMITH, ALISON. 'And woman created woman: Carswell, Shepherd and Muir, and the self-made woman.' *Gendering the nation,* edited Christopher Whyte. Edinburgh: University Press, 1995, p. 25-47.

Cathcart, Alex

MACPHERSON, HUGH. 'Alex Cathcart.' *Scottish Book Collector,* vol. 2, no. 4, [1990], p. 22-23.

Cleland, Mary

KYLE, ELISABETH. 'Mary Cleland.' *Scots Observer,* 23 July 1931, p. 4.

Cowan, Evelyn

COWAN, EVELYN. *Spring remembered: a Scottish Jewish childhood.* Edinburgh: Southside, 1974.

SIMPSON, ANNE. 'Portrait of Evelyn.' *Glasgow Herald,* 8 December 1976, p. 9.

Davidson, John

HUBBARD, TOM. 'John Davidson's Glasgow.' *Scottish Review,* no. 32, Nov. 1983, p. 13-19.

HUBBARD, TOM. 'The fiction of John Davidson'. *Studies in Scottish fiction: nineteenth century,* edited Horst W. Drescher and Joachim Schwend. Frankfurt: Peter Lang, 1985, p. 273-90.

Davis, Margaret Thomson

DAVIS, MARGARET THOMSON. *The making of a novelist.* Allison and Busby, 1982. Part autobiography, part advice to novice writers, with reference to her own methods of work.

LYONS, PATRICK. 'Margaret Thomson Davis.' *Dictionary of Literary Biography,* vol. 14, part 1. Detroit: Gale, [1982], p. 249-55.

Dolan, Chris

QUINN, DELILAH. 'Not magical, but marvellous reality.' *Scottish Book Collector,* vol. 5, no. 8, Spring 1997, p. 9-11.

Friel, George

WAUGH, AUBERON. 'Celtic twilights.' *Spectator,* 29 January 1972, p. 156-57. Review of *Mr Alfred MA,* notable for its patronising tone and for completely missing the point of the novel.

GARDNER, RAYMOND. 'A walk on the wild side.' *Guardian,* 24 March 1972, p. 12. A rare interview with Friel.

GILLESPIE, JAMES. 'Friel in the thirties.' *Edinburgh Review* 71, November 1985, p. 46-55. Memoir by a friend.

CAMERON, IAIN. *George Friel: an introduction to his life and work:* see 'Unpublished sources' above.

GIFFORD, DOUGLAS. 'Introduction.' *Mr Alfred MA*, Canongate Classics edition 1987, p. v-ix.

JARVIE, GORDON. 'Introduction.' *A friend of humanity.* Edinburgh: Polygon, 1992, p. [iii-xvi]. On Friel's short stories, collected for the first time in this volume.

Gaitens, Edward

WHYTE, HAMISH. *Edward Gaitens (1897-1966): a short bibliography.* Glasgow: The Mitchell Library, 1977.

Galloway, Janice

THOMAS, RUTH. 'Janice Galloway.' [interview] *Scottish Book Collector,* vol. 2, no. 6, August/September 1990, p. 2-3.

COOMBE, STELLA. 'Things Galloway.' [interview] *Harpies & Quines*, no. 1, May/June 1992, p. 26-29.

GALLOWAY, JANICE. 'Objective truth and the grinding machine or don't let the bastards etc. etc.' *Writers writing,* edited Jenny Brown and Shona Munro. Edinburgh: Mainstream, 1993, p. 73-77.

METZSTEIN, MARGERY. 'Of myths and men: aspects of gender in the fiction of Janice Galloway.' *The Scottish novel since the seventies,* edited Gavin Wallace and Randall Stevenson. Edinburgh: University Press, 1993, p. 136-46.

Galt, John

GORDON, IAN A. *John Galt: the life of a writer.* Edinburgh: Oliver and Boyd, 1972.

McCLURE, J.D. 'The language of *The entail.*' *Scottish Literary Journal,* vol. 8, no. 1, May 1981, p. 30-51.

Gray, Alasdair

A great deal of Gray criticism has appeared since 1981, and continues to appear. A useful list of major interviews and secondary reading is included in Crawford and Nairn: *The arts of Alasdair Gray* (1991) (see below). Only items not included there, or published after 1991, are listed here.

MURRAY, ISOBEL and TAIT, BOB. 'Alasdair Gray: *Lanark.*' *Ten modern Scottish novels.* Aberdeen: University Press, 1984, p. 219-39.

'Alasdair Gray.' *Contemporary Literary Criticism,* vol. 41. Detroit: Gale, [1987], p. 176-85. Reviews of *Lanark, Unlikely Stories, Mostly,* and *1982, Janine.*

CRAWFORD, ROBERT and NAIRN, THOM eds. *The arts of Alasdair Gray.* Edinburgh: University Press, 1991.

LUMSDEN, ALISON. 'Innovation and reaction in the fiction of Alasdair Gray.' *The Scottish novel since the seventies* (1993), *op. cit.,* p. 115-26.

MANLOVE, COLIN. *Scottish fantasy literature: a critical survey.* Edinburgh: Canongate Academic, 1994. See chapter 12 (p. 197-213) on *Lanark* and *Poor things.*

'The devil's audience' [interview with Gray]. *The Printer's Devil,* issue D, 1994, p. 15-34.

DALY, MACDONALD. 'Concplags and Totplag: *Lanark* exposed.' *Edinburgh Review 93,* Spring 1995, p. 166-200. Playful diatribe claiming that *Lanark* was in fact written by Daly's grandfather; with straight-faced response by Gray.

Review of Contemporary Fiction, vol. 15, no. 2, Summer 1995. Half of the issue (p. 103-98) is devoted to articles on Gray.

Glasgow Review, 3, Summer 1995. An issue devoted to Gray.

GRAY, ALASDAIR and CORDING, ALASTAIR. *Lanark.* [text of stage adaptation]. *Theatre Scotland,* vol. 4, no. 14, Summer 1995, p. 27-44. See also programme of tour (Glasgow: TAG Theatre Company, 1995) which contains articles on Gray, *Lanark* and Glasgow.

STENHOUSE, DAVID. 'A wholly healthy Scotland: a Reichian reading of *1982, Janine.*' *Edinburgh Review* 95, Spring 1996, p. 113-22.

Gunn, Neil M.

HART, F. R. and PICK, J. B. *Neil M. Gunn: a Highland life.* John Murray, 1981.

PRICE, RICHARD. *The fabulous matter of fact: the poetics of Neil M. Gunn.* Edinburgh: University Press, 1991.

McCULLOCH, MARGERY. 'Socialism and self-determination in the city novels of Neil Gunn.' *Chapman* 67, Winter 1991/92, p. 54-61.

Hamilton, Margaret

PORTER, DOROTHY. 'Ordinary lives.' *ScotLit* 5, Spring 1991, p. 3. Appreciation of her novel *Bull's penny.*

McMILLAN, DOROTHY PORTER. 'Margaret Hamilton: *The way they want it.*' *ScotLit* 7, Spring 1992, p. 3-4. On an unpublished novel set in mid-sixties Glasgow.

Hamilton, Thomas

LINDSAY, MAURICE. 'Soldier-writer: Thomas Hamilton (1789-1842).' *ScotLit 4,* Autumn 1990, p. 1.

Hanley, Clifford

HANLEY, CLIFFORD. *Dancing in the streets.* Hutchinson, 1958. Autobiographical: Glasgow childhood and adolescence in the 1920s and 1930s.

HEARN, SHEILA G. 'Cliff Hanley.' *Dictionary of Literary Biography,* vol. 14, part 2. Detroit: Gale, [1982], p. 377-80. Compares his novels as 'Clifford Hanley' and his thrillers published under the pseudonym 'Henry Calvin'.

Healy, Thomas

McGREGOR, KEN. 'From pickaxe to typewriter.' *Glasgow Herald,* 22 January 1977.

HEALY, THOMAS. *A hurting business.* Picador, 1996. Autobiography interwoven with boxing memoir.

Hendry, J. F.

Chapman 52, Spring 1988. A memorial issue with several articles on his life and work.

Hind, Archie

HIND, ARCHIE and TAIT, ROBERT. 'A novelist in Easterhouse.' *Scottish International,* no. 11, September 1970, p. 15-18.

HIND, ARCHIE. 'For Sadie.' *Scottish International,* vol. 6, no. 6, August 1973, p. 18-23. Extract from as yet unpublished novel.

MACPHERSON, HUGH. 'Archie Hind.' *Scottish Book Collector* 8, October/November 1988, p. 18-19.

Jenkins, Robin

JENKINS, ROBIN. 'Novelist in Scotland.' *Saltire Review,* vol. 2, no. 5, Autumn 1955, p. 7-10.

REID, ALEXANDER. 'The limits of charity:... a central theme in the novels of Robin Jenkins.' *Scotland's Magazine,* vol. 54, no. 10, October 1958, p. 43-44.

THOMPSON, ALASTAIR R. 'Faith and love: an examination of some themes in the novels of Robin Jenkins.' *New Saltire,* no. 3, Spring 1962, p. 57-64.

BURGESS, MOIRA. 'Robin Jenkins: a novelist of Scotland.' *Library Review,* vol. 22, no. 8, Winter 1970, p. 409-12.

BINDING, PAUL. 'Ambivalent patriot: the fiction of Robin Jenkins.' *New Edinburgh Review,* no. 53, February 1981, p. 20-22.

GIFFORD, DOUGLAS. '"God's colossal irony": Robin Jenkins and *Guests of war.' Cencrastus,* no. 24, Autumn 1986, p. 13-17. See also articles by Glenda Norquay (p. 3-6) and Bernard Sellin (p. 7-9).

MURRAY, ISOBEL. 'Introduction.' *Guests of war,* Scottish Academic Press edition 1988, p. vii-xxii.

MACPHERSON, HUGH. 'Robin Jenkins.' *Scottish Book Collector,* vol. 2, no. 1, August/ September 1989, p. 27-28.

Johnston, Henry

BROWN, D. WALKER. 'Henry Johnston.' *Clydeside litterateurs, op. cit.,* p. 99-106.

Kelman, James

This is a selective list of the extensive Kelman criticism in recent years. His later books have been widely reviewed; see in particular the many press features in October 1994 following the award of the Booker Prize to *How late it was, how late.*

WISEMAN, S. J. 'the curious nature of the practice.' *Edinburgh Review* 71, November 1985, p. 56-63.

McLEAN, DUNCAN. 'James Kelman interviewed.' *Edinburgh Review* 71, op. cit., p. 64-80.

MILLER, KARL. 'Glasgow Hamlet.' *Authors.* Oxford: Clarendon Press, 1989, p. 158-62.

McNEILL, KIRSTY. 'Interview with James Kelman.' *Chapman* 57, Summer 1989, p. 1-9.

'James Kelman.' *Contemporary Literary Criticism,* vol. 58. Detroit: Gale, [1990], p. 294-306. Reviews of his work to date.

GIFFORD, DOUGLAS. 'Discovering lost voices.' *Books in Scotland* 38, Summer 1991, p. 1-6.

KELMAN, JAMES. 'The importance of Glasgow in my work.' *Some recent attacks.* Stirling: AK Press, 1992, p. 78-84.

CRAIG, CAIRNS. 'Resisting arrest: James Kelman.' *The Scottish novel since the seventies*

(1993), *op.cit.,* p. 99-114.

MALEY, WILLY. 'Swearing blind: Kelman and the curse of the working classes.' *Edinburgh Review* 95, Spring 1996, p. 105-12. On the question of 'bad language' in Kelman, particularly *How late it was, how late.*

McCORMICK, MICHAEL. 'For Jimmy Kelboats.' *Chapman 83,* [Summer 1996], p. 30-34.

Kennaway, James

AITCHISON, JAMES. 'The novels of James Kennaway.' *Scottish Review,* no. 21, February 1981, p. 40-45.

MASSIE, ALLAN. 'The artful art of James Kennaway.' *New Edinburgh Review anthology,* edited James Cameron. Edinburgh: Polygon, 1982, p. 124-35.

Kennedy, A. L.

THOMAS, RUTH. 'A. L. Kennedy.' [interview] *Scottish Book Collector,* vol. 3, no. 12, August/ September 1993, p. 2-4.

SMITH, ALISON. 'Four success stories.' *Chapman 74-75,* Autumn/Winter 1993, p. 177-92.

CLOSE, AJAY. 'A L right now.' *Scotland on Sunday: Spectrum,* 23 January 1994, p. 3.

KELLAWAY, KATE. 'The blurred angel's story.' *Observer Review,* 30 January 1994, p.18.

GLOVER, GILLIAN. 'Call me A. L.' *Scotsman,* 1 December 1995.

ADAIR, TOM. 'Danger woman.' *Scotland on Sunday: Spectrum,* 19 January 1997, p. 11.

Kuppner, Frank

CRAWFORD, ROBERT. 'Frank Kuppner in the 1980s.' *Scottish Literary Journal,* vol. 17, no. 2, November 1990, p. 58-74.

THOMAS, RUTH. 'Frank Kuppner.' *Scottish Book Collector,* vol. 3, no. 8, December/January 1992/1993, p. 2-3.

McArthur, Alexander

McARTHUR, ALEXANDER. 'Why I wrote *No mean city.' Daily Record,* 1 November 1935, p. 7. Expresses McArthur's intention to 'put the poorest of Glasgow's citizens on the map'.

DAMER, SEAN. 'No mean writer? The curious case of Alexander McArthur.' *A Glasgow collection,* edited Kevin McCarra and Hamish Whyte. Glasgow: City Libraries, 1990, p. 25-42. Pieces together hitherto uncollected information on McArthur's life, death and writing career.

MacColla, Fionn

MORRISON, DAVID ed. *Essays on Fionn MacColla.* Thurso: Caithness Books, 1973.

McCrone, Guy

McCRONE, GUY. 'Guy McCrone.' *Scottish Field,* March 1952, p. 36. Notes on the genesis and writing of *Wax fruit* and its sequels.

MacDougall, Carl

GIFFORD, DOUGLAS. 'MacDougall's Glasgow.' *Books in Scotland* 33, [1990], p. 1-4. Interview on MacDougall's involvement with the exhibition 'Glasgow's Glasgow', and on current Glasgow writing.

MacDOUGALL, CARL. 'Relative strangers.' *Scotsman: Weekend,* 10 August 1996, p. 16-19. On his childhood and relatives in Oban.

McGILLIVRAY, ALAN. 'Interview with Carl MacDougall.' *Laverock,* [2, October 1996], p. 9-17.

MacGill, Patrick

DAY, A. E. 'From Irish navvy to royal librarian.' *Library World,* vol. 71, no. 831, September 1969, p. 68-72.

MITCHELL, JACK. 'Patrick MacGill.' *Scottish Marxist,* no. 6, April 1974, p. 41-4. Part of 'The struggle for the working-class novel in Scotland', *op.cit.*

ASPINWALL, BERNARD. 'Patrick MacGill: the voice of the Irish, British and universal man.' *Contemporary Review* 258, June 1991, p. 320-25.

ANDERSON, FREDDY. 'Patrick MacGill: an Irish literary career in Scotland.' *Cencrastus* 55, Autumn 1996, p. 22-23.

McGinn, Matt

McGINN, MATT. *McGinn of the Calton.* Glasgow: District Libraries, 1987. Includes autobiographical writing, songs and poems, and stories.

McIlvanney, William

McILVANNEY, WILLIAM. 'Growing up in the west.' *Memoirs of a modern Scotland*, edited Karl Miller. Faber and Faber, 1970, p. 168-78.

CRAIG, CAIRNS. 'William McIlvanney.' *Dictionary of Literary Biography*, vol. 14 part 2. Detroit: Gale, [1982], p. 508-10.

'Inhabiting the paradox: William McIlvanney.' [interview] *Radical Scotland*, October/November 1984, p. 24-27.

CRAIG, CAROL. 'Men and women in McIlvanney's fiction.' *Edinburgh Review* 73, May 1986, p. 42-49.

'William McIlvanney.' *Contemporary Literary Criticism*, vol. 42. Detroit: Gale, [1987], p. 279-86. Reviews of his novels to date.

DIXON, KEITH. 'Writing on the borderline.' *Studies in Scottish Literature,* 24 (1989), p. 142-57.

'William McIlvanney talks to Douglas Gifford.' [interview] *Books in Scotland* 30, Spring 1989, p. 1-4.

DENTITH, SIMON. '"This shitty urban machine humanised": the urban crime novel and the novels of William McIlvanney.' *Watching the detectives: essays on crime fiction*, edited Ian A. Bell and Graham Daldry. Macmillan, 1990, p. 18-36.

McILVANNEY, WILLIAM. *Surviving the shipwreck.* Edinburgh: Mainstream, 1991. Collected essays: see in particular 'The courage of our doubts', p. 153-62 (on *Laidlaw*) and 'A shield against the Gorgon', p. 217-38 (on his intention to reflect working-class experience).

McILVANNEY, WILLIAM. 'Together to the death.' *Scotsman,* 30 November 1992.

DICKSON, BETH. 'Class and being in the novels of William McIlvanney.' *The Scottish novel since the seventies* (1993), *op.cit.,* p. 54-70.

McGILLIVRAY, ALAN. 'Natural loyalties: the work of William McIlvanney.' *Laverock,* [no. 1, February 1995], p. 13-24.

McILVANNEY, WILLIAM. 'Plato in a boiler suit.' *Scottish writers talking,* edited Isobel Murray and Bob Tait. Phantassie: Tuckwell Press, 1996, p. 132-54. Interview recorded in 1984.

Macmillan, Archibald

BROWN, D. WALKER. 'Archibald Macmillan (Jeems Kaye).' *Clydeside litterateurs, op.cit,* p. 138-46.

'The passing of "Jeems Kaye".' *The Bailie,* 12 August 1925, p. 9. Obituary and evaluation.

Mills, George

Letters from George Mills to George Cruickshank: see 'Unpublished sources' above.

'Men you know – no 299.' *The Bailie,* no. 299, 10 July 1878, p. 1-3.

Morrison family

HUNTER, STEWART. 'The Morrisons.' *Scots Magazine,* new series, vol. 59, no. 3, June 1953, p. 187-92. On 'the writing Morrisons', the family which included the novelists Nancy Brysson Morrison, March Cost and T. J. Morrison.

Muir, Edwin

MUIR, EDWIN. *An autobiography.* Hogarth Press, 1954. Revised and expanded edition of *The story and the fable* (1940); see chapter 3, 'Glasgow', with reference to *Poor Tom.*

BUTTER, P. H. *Edwin Muir.* Edinburgh: Oliver and Boyd, 1962. Includes a fuller treatment of *Poor Tom* than does his longer *Edwin Muir: man and poet* (1966).

REID, ALEXANDER. 'Eden and the boneyard: a note on the life and work of Edwin Muir, poet, critic, novelist and mystic.' *Scotland's Magazine,* vol. 58, no. 6, June 1962, p. 47-48.

Munro, Hugh

CONN, STEWART. '*The Clydesiders* by Hugh Munro.' *New Saltire* 3, Spring 1962, p. 95-96.

BIGGAR, JOAN. 'The man behind Clutha.' *Scots Magazine,* new series, vol. 107, no. 3, June 1977, p. 254-59.

Munro, Neil

MUNRO, NEIL. *The brave days: a chronicle from the north.* Edinburgh: Porpoise Press, 1931. See particularly the valuable biographical introduction by George Blake.

OSBORNE, BRIAN D. 'The unknown Munro.' *Scottish Book Collector,* vol. 3, no. 11, June/July 1993, p. 9-11. The editor of new editions of the Para Handy, Erchie and Jimmy Swan stories considers that 'all three have strong connections with Glasgow, that great all-consuming city'.

Nicolson, Robert

BENEDICTUS, DAVID. 'Last things first.' *Radio Times,* 31 October 1974, p. 22-23. A rare interview with the author of *Mrs Ross.*

Niven, Frederick

GRIEVE, C. M. 'Frederick Niven: J. J. Bell.' Chapter 10 in *Contemporary Scottish studies* (1926), *op.cit.*

ADCOCK, ST JOHN. 'Frederick Niven.' *The glory that was Grub Street.* Sampson Low, Marston [1928], p. 247-57. Memoir of Niven before his emigration to Canada.

Letters of R. B. Cunninghame Graham to Frederick Niven: see 'Unpublished sources' above.

NIVEN, FREDERICK. *Coloured spectacles.* Collins, 1938. Autobiography.

DUNLOP, JOHN. 'The spirit of Niven.' *Scottish Field,* vol. 102, no. 623, November 1954, p. 45.

REID, ALEXANDER. 'A Scottish Chekhov?' *Scotland's Magazine*, vol. 58, no. 3, March 1962, p. 45-46.

WALKER, JOHN. '"Scotland is a kingdom of the mind": the novels of Frederick Niven.' *Studies in Scottish Literature*, vol. 24, 1989, p. 92-106.

NEW, W. H. 'Frederick John Niven.' *Dictionary of Literary Biography*, vol. 92. Detroit: Gale, 1990, p. 271-75.

BURGESS, MOIRA. 'The Glasgow novels of Frederick Niven.' *Scottish Book Collector,* vol. 3, no. 3, February/March 1992, p. 14-15.

Reid, John Macnair

BURGESS, MOIRA. 'A Glasgow novel.' *Library Review,* vol. 22, no. 7, Autumn 1970, p. 391. Review of *Judy from Crown Street.*

Roy, George

'Men you know – no. 92.' *The Bailie,* no. 92, 22 July 1874, p. 1-2.

Scott, Walter

GEORGE, J. F. 'Bailie Nicol Jarvie: who he was and what he was. An attempt at a biographical appreciation.' *The Bailie,* 15 December 1922, p. 79-83. A spoof biography and genealogy.

SPENCE, LEWIS. 'Bailie Nicol Jarvie: an inimitable pen-picture.' *SMT Magazine,* vol. 8, no. 4, April 1932, p. 53-54.

Sharp, Alan

'Alan Sharp's journey.' *Scottish International,* vol. 5, no. 1, January 1972, p. 20-28.

Spence, Alan

SPENCE, ALAN. 'Boom baby.' *Jock Tamson's bairns,* edited Trevor Royle. Hamish Hamilton, 1977, p. 14-28.

MASSIE, ALLAN. 'Sense and sensibility.' *Weekend Scotsman,* 27 August 1977, p. 2. Long review of *Its colours they are fine.*

SPENCE, ALAN. 'Regrets? I've had a few, but then again…' *Scotsman,* 19 May 1990. 'Why *The magic flute* took so long to write.'

BURNS, JOHN. 'Mastering the magic flute.' *Cencrastus* 38, Winter 1990/91, p. 41-42.

Torrington, Jeff

'Jeff Torrington in conversation with Jim Kelman.' *West Coast Magazine* 12, [January 1993], p. 18-21.

McLEAN, DUNCAN. 'Jeff Torrington.' [interview] *Scottish Book Collector,* vol. 3, no. 1, April/May 1993, p. 2-3.

Trocchi, Alexander

CAMPBELL, JAMES. 'Alexander Trocchi.' *Dictionary of Literary Biography,* vol. 15. Detroit: Gale, [1983], p. 538-41.

Edinburgh Review 70, August 1985. A Trocchi feature (p. 32-65) includes articles by John Calder, Tom McGrath, Edwin Morgan and Christopher Logue.

SCOTT, ANDREW MURRAY. *Alexander Trocchi: the making of the monster.* Edinburgh: Polygon, 1991.

Tytler, Sarah

'DOGBERRY'. 'Saint Mungo's city.' *Quiz,* 15 August 1884, p. 230.

'Henrietta Keddie ("Sarah Tytler").' *Scots Pictorial,* 1 January 1898, p. 354-55.

KEDDIE, HENRIETTA. *Three generations: the story of a middle-class Scottish family.* John Murray, 1911. Autobiography, partly devoted to earlier family history.

The Glasgow Novel: a survey

1 Before 1870: Forerunners of the Glasgow Novel

The Glasgow novel is almost, though not entirely, a late-Victorian creation. The first edition of this bibliography dealt only with novels published since 1870 and depicting Glasgow from that time on, and when this limitation was removed in later editions it was found that comparatively few titles had to be added at the early end of the chronological index.

Some of these few, however, deserve mention in this introduction to the Glasgow novel, because in them may be seen a foreshadowing of certain recurring themes in later Glasgow fiction: the Glasgow merchant, the strong Glasgow woman, the urban kailyard, and the slums.

If the most memorable fictional evocation of eighteenth-century Glasgow is Scott's description of the Cathedral in *Rob Roy* (1817), close behind it comes the night-piece in the Tolbooth, and this forms our introduction to Bailie Nicol Jarvie, regarded as the epitome of the Glasgow merchant. In one aspect of his character at least (for it would be wrong to overlook his inheritance from 'the auld wife ayont the fire at Stuckavrallachan') he embodies the hard-headed, unromantic Glasgow businessman, and may be seen as an ancestor of the sturdy, well-doing heroes – if 'hero' is not a word they would deplore as applied to themselves – in some of the most convincing Glasgow novels of later years.

We think of Tam Drysdale, dyer and calico-printer, in Sarah Tytler's *St Mungo's city* (1884); the men of the textile warehouses around Ingram Street, given almost documentary treatment by Frederick Niven in *Justice of the peace* (1914) and *The staff at Simson's* (1937); John Mungo, taking the classic route from pedlar to wealthy businessman, in George Woden's *Mungo* (1932); and Arthur Moorhouse, depicted in business, home and society in Guy McCrone's *Wax fruit* (1947) and its sequels. Their world is Victorian and Edwardian Glasgow in its commercial heyday, but the ancestor of that city is the prosperous eighteenth-century town observed by Frank Osbaldistone, and the ancestor of these level-headed men is the careful and industrious Bailie Nicol Jarvie.

John Galt's *The entail* (1822) is regarded as his 'Glasgow novel', and Claud Walkinshaw is another of our early Glasgow merchants, but his wife, the splendid Leddy o' Grippy, is also a forerunner in her own right. It may be objected that her particular breed of old Scottish lady is not a specifically Glasgow type, flourishing as strongly, and more remarked upon, in eighteenth-century Edinburgh; yet we see Glasgow ladies in *The entail* who compare with the famed 'directresses' of Edinburgh balls.

The Glasgow novel as it later develops is rich in strong female characters. Typically they are middle-aged women, mothers or grandmothers, supporting ineffectual husbands or unsatisfactory families. Bel Moorhouse of *Wax fruit* comes to mind because this is precisely her picture of herself, but in fact social conventions, and her quiet but strong-minded husband, keep her matriarchal tendencies under control, and the genuine Glasgow matron in *Wax fruit* is Bel's widowed mother Mrs Barrowfield.

But she and the Leddy o' Grippy, comfortably off, have little enough to tax their sharp minds and organising ability. The same qualities, in later Glasgow novels, are exhibited at a lower social level and in face of the major problems of war or unemployment. It is not suggested that these later authors owe anything, even indirectly, to Galt, but we may certainly note the recurrence of the strong-minded woman, impelled by pride and love of her family, the centre of her household. Danny Shields's feckless wife Agnes in Blake's *The shipbuilders* (1935) is an exception, untypical (at least in fiction) of the women of the depression years; the more representative figure is Julia, the mother in Hugh Munro's *The Clydesiders* (1961). We may cite also Grannie in John Macnair Reid's *Judy from Crown Street* (1970), a complex character of love and hasty spite; the calm, almost saintly Bell McShelvie in Robin Jenkins's *Guests of war* (1956); and the definitely too good to be true Meg Macrae in Clifford Hanley's *Another street, another dance* (1983).

This strong woman character, so distinctively recurrent in Glasgow fiction, is the Leddy o' Grippy transmuted. It may just be noted that these are all depicted by male writers with filial love and admiration, and that a slightly different view – of women equally strong who yet know that they could crack, and sometimes do – is supplied by such novels as Catherine Carswell's *Open the door!* (1920), Dot Allan's *Makeshift* (1928), and the continuing work of Agnes Owens, Janice Galloway and A. L. Kennedy.

At first sight Mrs Young, narrator of George Roy's *Generalship* (1858), may appear to be another of the strong, directing women of Glasgow fiction; like Bel Moorhouse, she certainly is so in her own estimation. She is, however, a caricature of the type. The triteness and self-satisfied tone of her narration mark her out rather as a forerunner of what we shall be calling the 'urban kailyard' school which flourished in the early years of the twentieth century (at which time *Generalship*, evidently popular, was still in print). The book's episodic structure, its interspersed Scots dialect, its heavy sentimentality, its unquestioning acceptance of establishment views, and its preoccupation with domestic affairs are all marks of the kailyard. It is Mrs Young's ambition to see her John a town councillor at least, with 'Bailie Young' the eventual goal, and as she counsels her readers 'to seek, in their respective circumstances, contentment – the only certain source of happiness', we may identify the absence of self-analysis also typical of kailyard characters. Some sharp and ironic short stories by George Roy, however, lead us to suspect that he could analyse Mrs Young very well, and that she is not so much an example as a parody of the attitudes which would earnestly flower in the urban kailyard a little later on.

George Mills's two-volume novel *The beggar's benison* (1866) combines to some extent features of both the mercantile novel and the urban kailyard school. Its nameless hero follows a traditional path from office-boy to successful businessman, while his personal history is as romantically unlikely as the kailyard could desire. The starting-point for this odyssey, however, is the Rookery, a slum tenement in the Goosedubbs of Glasgow, and here the descriptions are matter-of-fact, detailed, and at times startlingly macabre. It is an early representation of the slums and underworld of Glasgow, an ambience which recurs throughout Glasgow fiction, sometimes realistically and sometimes with sensational intent.

The hero's attitude, too, is one found in later novels: he revisits the Goosedubbs as an adult, not from philanthropic motives but 'only… impelled by curiosity to know if it still existed…' This reasonable curiosity satisfied, he sets out to make his fortune, accepting the Goosedubbs as a fact of life; as do very many later novels touching on the subject of the slums.

2   The Historical Novel and the Victorian Tract

If we reserve the term 'historical novel' for one written about a period of which the writer has no first-hand knowledge, there were until recently strangely few historical novels about Glasgow. The early days of the city, up to the mid-nineteenth century, had been almost neglected by novelists, and although the Victorian period has always been well documented in Glasgow fiction, some writers, like Frederick Niven, were in fact describing the scenes of their youth. Things have changed with the advent of popular novelists like Margaret Thomson Davis and Jessica Stirling, who have used as background, as well as the depression years of their early childhood, the more distant and (as perceived) more colourful days of the eighteenth-century tobacco lords and the Victorian captains of industry and trade.

Nothing in this genre has yet quite replaced Guy McCrone's *Wax fruit* (1947). With its sequels *Aunt Bel* (1949) and *The Hayburn family* (1952), it follows the fortunes of the Moorhouses and Hayburns, prosperous merchants and engineers, from 1870 to 1901. In its almost Galsworthian plan, Arthur and Bel Moorhouse are at the centre of an intricate web of family relationships, but we do not forget Arthur's brothers Mungo and David, or his young half-sister Phoebe, married to Henry Hayburn. Carefully chosen but not overwhelming details – the files of *The Glasgow Herald* have been skilfully employed – build up a picture of Victorian Glasgow in a series of vivid imaginative descriptions.

McCrone's real achievement is to breathe life into the formal portraits in which our Victorian grandparents are enshrined. Bel Moorhouse – innocently snobbish, socially ambitious but warm-hearted – is his best creation, and with Arthur she is shown to be endearingly young and human. The passionate youthful marriage of the younger couple Phoebe and Henry Hayburn is interestingly explored, and their early years in Vienna extend the scope of *Wax fruit* beyond the slightly constricted bounds of the Moorhouse world. Probably *Wax fruit* in essence is not so much a picture of Glasgow, nor even of Bel Moorhouse, but of that now almost unimaginable institution, the Victorian family.

It is, as we have indicated, a middle-class family, set mainly in respectable old town houses and the rising West End. Yet there is one glimpse of the other side of Victorian Glasgow, in the nightmarish sequence where young Phoebe enters the slums of the Saltmarket to rescue Bel's small son, enticed away from his nurse. The experience is a shocking and enlightening one for Phoebe; almost more shocking to us is the way the episode is discreetly hushed up by the family, so that the genteel social round may continue undisturbed. This Victorian attitude towards slum-dwellers is briefly acknowledged by McCrone, though not condemned:

Arthur was well used to the look of these people. As a rule he accepted them, telling himself, as all his like did, that do what one would, poverty and squalor would always be.

Contemporary fiction tends to confirm that here too McCrone had done his homework. Just as the hero of *The beggar's benison* returned to the Goosedubbs to see if the slums of his childhood really existed, we find the young heroine of C. M. Gordon's *Jet Ford* (1880) making a similar pilgrimage before departing for the mission field and respectable marriage:

The place had not altered much. Children, as poor and hopeless-looking as Jet had been herself, played away, heedless of their misery.

But not really hopeless, because:

Jet knew and rejoiced in the thought that the sinful, the poor and the young were far better cared for than they had been when she was a child… Bands of Christian workers gathered in the young… Band of Hope meetings… and Penny Savings Banks… had sprung up in all directions.

It is a present-day viewpoint which suggests to us that the Victorians, as well as throwing up savings banks, might have thought of pulling down the slums; yet we find in these same Victorian tracts some stirring of common sense as well as compassion. William Naismith's *City echoes* (1884), though a conventional 'waif' story, has a distinctly more sympathetic outlook than the previous works we have quoted. There are some pertinent remarks on the duty of the School Board to find, house and teach homeless children, voiced not by a distant philanthropist, but by a member of the 'respectable working class' (slightly 'higher up in the social formation' than the outcasts of the slums), and by the matter-of-fact City Missionary who befriends the waif Jim.

The contrast between these practical people who actually work in the slums, and the *nouveau riche* hero of *The beggar's benison* thankfully putting his past behind him, is clear enough. Along with Arthur Moorhouse, comfortably accepting the status quo 'as all his like did', it should perhaps be borne in mind as we turn next to the strange fact that, for many Scottish novelists in the decades around the turn of the century, these notorious slums might not have existed at all.

3 The Kailyard and the Industrial Novel

A recurring complaint in criticism of Scottish fiction of the late nineteenth and early twentieth centuries has been the lack of what we may call the industrial novel: the novel set in a modern city or large industrial town, having for theme, or at least background, the problems and conflicts of urban society. The perceived absence of such novels is seen as particularly remarkable in view of the immense industrial expansion in the central belt of Scotland during the later nineteenth century.

The effect of this expansion on the size and ethnic make-up of Glasgow alone is well documented. The population of the city more than doubled between 1851 and 1901, and in 1881 seventeen per cent of that population had been born in Ireland or in the crofting counties of north and west Scotland. Little imagination is required to picture these immigrants, bringing a rich strain of Celtic blood to the sturdily independent city of Bailie Nicol Jarvie's descendants, many of them crowded into grossly inadequate housing and tied down to uncongenial jobs. The situation would appear potentially rich in conflict and drama, and it would seem reasonable to expect some reflection of this in the fiction of the closing years of the nineteenth century.

Recent research by William Donaldson (see our reading list) has found that 'city novels' were in fact being written, appearing in serial form in newspapers and periodicals, but that, since few of them attained book publication, they escaped the notice of critics and of the (largely middle-class) book-reading public. It remains true to some extent, therefore, that the 1880s and 1890s in Scottish fiction are the years of the Kailyard School. This movement too is undergoing some re-evaluation, but we may make the general point that the Kailyarders, rather than looking around them at the already urban and industrialised Scotland of their day, persistently looked back to a rural Scotland of small towns and villages, where the parish pump, rather than the factory chimney, held the centre of the scene.

We have noticed, however, the appearance, before the blossoming of the Kailyard, of the hard-headed Glasgow merchant in the person of Bailie Nicol Jarvie, and of an early picture of the notorious Glasgow slums in *The beggar's benison*. These two lines of development – as well as the 'urban kailyard' school, which we shall discuss soon – bridge the Kailyard period in Glasgow fiction.

We left the typical merchant, as personified by Bailie Nicol Jarvie, in the middle years of the eighteenth century. In Sarah Tytler's *St Mungo's city* (1884) he makes his reappearance, now unmistakably a Victorian man of business. The commercial expansion of the city is well under way, and one of its kingpins is Tam Drysdale. He is a calico-printer, a self-made man, who has worked his way up to become sole proprietor of what was once a family business. The intricacies of this lost inheritance, pursued through wills and marriage contracts with a pertinacity reminiscent of *The entail*, form a main strand of the plot.

Basically, however, *St Mungo's city* is the long, leisurely, but far from uneventful story of two families. We meet first the three Miss Mackinnons, Glasgow gentlewomen surely in a clear line of descent from Galt's ladies, and in fact great-granddaughters of a tobacco lord. They are reduced to utter poverty, hanging on in expectation of a long-delayed legacy; but they are indomitable old ladies, and when the will, eventually made public, does not please them, they just burn it.

The Drysdales' son and daughters, if a little more conventional than these splendid ladies, nevertheless furnish the material for a genuinely appealing novel of manners; and in the son, young Tam, there is a distinct spark of originality. We meet him as a somewhat dour, awkward young man, college-educated but unwilling to do anything definite with his life. The trouble proves to lie in the first stirrings of a social conscience, from which, however, he recovers well before the end of the story. His fellow-feeling for the working classes is sadly shaken when he joins them on a Clyde steamer trip 'doon the watter' to Rothesay at the Glasgow Fair. The chapter is a fine piece of observation, adding notably to the book's general picture of a bustling, enthusiastic, attractively naive Victorian Glasgow.

The city and its business world have moved on and grown up a little by the turn of the century, the setting date of Frederick Niven's *Justice of the peace* (1914). The feeling of mercantile adventure has ebbed a little and the soft-goods warehouse of Ebenezer Moir is a settled family firm with its own routine, tradition and characters. Not the least of the book's virtues is its accurate and humorous rendering of warehouse conversation, and Niven, once an art student, has also an exceptionally good eye for the Glasgow scene, many of his descriptions being visually brilliant.

Yet the essence of *Justice of the peace* is in its treatment of a complex set of family emotions. The husband-wife, mother-son relationships are well handled, given the pathological jealousy which afflicts Mrs Moir; but the father-son relationship is treated with the greatest sensitivity and originality. The situation is classic to the point of being hackneyed: the artistic boy destined by his father to go into the family business. The reader is prepared to sympathise with Martin, the son, and to look on him as the hero of the book, but Niven did not choose his novel's title at random. The justice of the peace, the big straightforward manufacturer Ebenezer Moir, is in fact the main character, and the surprise is that he is immensely appealing. It is notoriously difficult to make a character both likeable and interesting: Niven succeeds, and produces in *Justice of the peace* a well-rounded novel which deserves to be better known than it now is.

Patrick MacGill's two earliest novels, *Children of the dead end* (1914) and *The rat-pit* (1915), are contemporary with *Justice of the peace*, but describe a Glasgow very different from Ebenezer Moir's. These are parallel novels, telling the story of Dermod Flynn, an Irish navvy, and his sweetheart Norah Ryan, in their separate odysseys from Ireland to Scotland in search of work. The first book is told from Dermod's viewpoint and the second from Norah's, a device which has been used by much more consciously stylistic novelists.

Our concern here is with the Glasgow sequences, set in the grim slums through which Dermod searches for Norah. These passages form a minor part of *Children of the dead end*, but in *The rat-pit* the slum sequences are of major importance. 'The rat-pit' is a female lodging-house where Norah stays briefly, but MacGill explains in his Introduction:

The underworld… has always appeared to me as a Greater Rat-pit… It is in this larger sense that I have chosen the name for the title of Norah Ryan's story.

Though the novel has sentimental passages, the description is realistic to a degree startling at this early date. We have certainly noted descriptions of the slums in what I

George Roy
The Bailie, 22 July 1874

Sarah Tytler
Fife News Almanac, 1905. Courtesy of
University of St Andrews Library

Archibald Macmillan
D. Walker Brown, *Clydeside Litterateurs*, 1897

Frederick Niven
Scotland's Magazine, March 1962

have called the 'Victorian tracts', but MacGill's treatment has the air of something observed and experienced from the vagrant's point of view, not from that of the social reformer. Moreover, the writers of the tracts, as we have seen, praise the reformers' attempts to set the slum-dwellers on the straight and narrow, without apparently considering the desirability of abolishing the slums. MacGill has a clear intention:

> *The rat-pit* is a transcript from life… Some may think that such things should not be written about; but public opinion, like the light of day, is a great purifier, and to hide a sore from the surgeon's eye out of miscalled delicacy is surely a supreme folly.

We have not so far mentioned John Blair's *Jean* (1906), in spite of its early date, simply because it stands alone and is difficult to relate to either the mercantile novel or the slum school. Much less, however, can it be aligned with the urban kailyard novels which are its contemporaries. 'John Blair' is a pseudonym and his (or her) identity has not been established. We do not know where *Jean* comes from.

It is a short book, with a plot which, baldly retold, appears hackneyed in its simplicity. Jean, a factory girl, falls in love with and is seduced by the handsome stranger Jock; she enters upon the inevitable downward process, becomes a prostitute, is rescued by her faithful first love Hughie, and dies of consumption. Such a summary, however, does no justice to the novel's unsentimental yet unsensational realism and its quite unpatronising view of working-class life. Jean is a girl of spirit, dealing competently with her drunken father's threats, and Glasgow courtship, in the earlier, more light-hearted parts of the story, is portrayed with humour and sympathy. But the most remarkable passage is her mother's advice when Jean's pregnancy is revealed:

> 'I was like you, an' I merriet the man, but if I had it tae dae ower again, I wadna leeve the life I've led for a' the jewels in Windsor Castle. Jean, if ye want my advice, hae yer wean, an' if need be, work for it… Never mind whit folk'll say. It'll blaw ower in a week. The ither wey, tak my word for it, 'll be for life.'

The calm, humane sense of this is hardly matched in Glasgow fiction until we reach the modern realists of the 'twenties and 'thirties; and we should repeat that its date is 1906, in the midst of the coy evasions and sentimentality of the urban kailyard.

These half-dozen novels cannot quite be said to form a school of industrial fiction, particularly when they stand as isolated examples in a period of some forty years, and we are still left with this strange blind spot in Scottish fiction, the ignoring by most novelists of the urban and industrial scene in favour of the rural and parochial. The causes of this phenomenon have been variously identified. We may consider as possible reasons, for instance, the exceptionally swift and brutal impact of the Industrial Revolution, with, as it were, a stupefying effect on contemporary writers; the influence of Scott's novels with their historical-romantic view of Scotland; and a desire to record, with perhaps more enthusiasm than accuracy, the picturesque elements of an obsolescent way of life.

Another suggested reason is the predominance among contemporary novelists of the middle-class, comfortably off, reasonably educated, established section of the community. Scott, for instance, was a lawyer; 'Ian Maclaren' (John Watson) and S. R. Crockett, pillars of the Kailyard School, were Free Church ministers; Barrie, an adherent of the same church, though the son of a weaver, was a university graduate and a journalist. The voice of the working class in that group of writers is simply not heard, and we may probably agree that Kailyard writers were not personally involved in the problems of the slums and the factories. It may be a broad generalisation, but given the evidence it is certainly tempting, to say that they were happy to leave matters as they stood. This is the attitude which comes through in much Glasgow fiction of the time.

A clear expression of middle-class self-satisfaction, for example, is heard in *Martha Spreull* by 'Zachary Fleming' (Henry Johnston), published as early as 1884. Since this is a light book intended as entertainment, we ought perhaps to give Martha the benefit of the doubt and assume that she is being satirical; if so, there is presumably an attitude abroad for her to satirise. She casts a disapproving eye on an early city improvement scheme:

Eh me! sic a changed place… Hale streets hae been dung doon, and fine new anes wi' bonnie big lands o' hooses planted in their place… I mind when I lived in George Street, whenever I became discontented wi' myself or my hoose, I just took a walk doon the High Street and back by Bell's Wynd. It was a grand cure, for I aye saw sae muckle dirt and misery there that I generally cam' hame thankfu' and happy…

We can see little indication of a social conscience here.

Neil Munro's *Erchie* (1904) allows its hero to remark on 'the auld-established and justly-popular slum hoose'. Again we may hope that Erchie at that point had his tongue in his cheek, frequently though he is presented as a fount of pawky folk wisdom. That is all we can offer to explain away his words a few lines later:

'Slums! wha wants to abolish slums?… If there werena folk leevin' in slums I couldna buy chape shirts… *The slums'll no' touch ye if ye don't gang near them.*' (my italics)

John Cockburn in *Tenement* (1925) sees that the segregation desired by Erchie is far from complete:

A suburb populated mainly by shipyard toilers and their incidentals, with, of course, a percentage of city workers who have been taught to regard the district as a desirable residential and healthy district. Of poverty and modest comfort evenly distributed. Dismal tenements and miserable cottages. Bright new tenements and trim villas…

Perhaps we may see here at last some evidence of a developing social conscience in Scottish fiction, and even refer it to a similar trend in public consciousness. It is a truism that the old order of the Victorians and Edwardians went down in the breakers of the First World War. Not quite so readily in 1925 as in 1884 would even 'auld Tam' Drysdale (of *St Mungo's city*) have counselled his idealistic son, 'We're not here to mend the whole economy of things.' By the 'twenties it was beginning to be felt that we were there for exactly that purpose.

It is therefore not so surprising to find that writers of 'the Glasgow school' – including Dot Allan, George Blake, John Carruthers, Catherine Carswell and John Cockburn, who all produced their first novels between 1920 and 1925 – must be considered in a separate section of this essay. Some of these writers, as we shall see, are perhaps more workmanlike than inspired, and their early novels have the faults of youth, but they attempt to look at contemporary Glasgow, rather than retreating to the gentler and unreal surroundings of the kailyard.

4   The Urban Kailyard and the Gangland School

Before considering what may now be called the realistic school, we should look at two of its near contemporaries, which in a sense lie at opposite ends of realism: the *urban kailyard* and the *gangland* schools. The very fact that it is easy to assign many Glasgow novels to one or other of these categories should put us on our guard; the simplicity of attitude and treatment which makes their recognition fairly straightforward is not generally an attribute of a major novel, and we shall find more substance and significance in novels not so readily classifiable. There is, however, some interest in the existence of these two well-marked conventions.

Why do we treat the two schools side by side, when the superficial difference between them is so great? The first is a projection in urban terms of the 'sweet, amusing little stories of bucolic intrigue' (to quote the memorable words of George Blake) which have been briefly dealt with earlier. The urban kailyard grew up contemporaneously with the true (rural) Kailyard School, though it reached its full flower a little later; like its rural version it survives today, unconsidered by literary critics but popular with a large, mainly female, readership. The second, appearing in the 1920s, reaching its apotheosis in 1935 with McArthur and Long's *No mean city*, and continuing with a number of inferior imitations, lies at the other end of the scale of realism, though one or two novels (for instance, the early works of Hugh C. Rae) show the possibility of striking a balance. If, at the height of the Kailyard's popularity, the population of Scotland might seem overweighted with ministers, dominies, pawky weavers and consumptive students, *No mean city*, and particularly its descendants, evoke a community equally crowded with gangsters, hard men and loose women.

This one-sided view of life is the great fault which these two schools share. No community – much less a city the size of Glasgow – consists of nothing but bourgeois or nothing but unemployed; a strength of some of the better, and genuinely realistic, Glasgow novels is their recognition of this.

But more important to the novelist than the complexity of a community is the complexity of the individual human soul, and the writers of these two schools are sadly ready to ignore this, or not to recognise it in the first place. Broadly speaking, in the kailyard people are good (or at worst comic) while in gangland people are bad (or at best contemptible). The better pieces of writing in both schools, those tending to rise by design or chance into something less stereotyped and more like life, do make some attempt to show the other side of the coin. Neil Munro's Erchie, the pawkiest waiter in fiction, comes across most of the time as a genuine urban kailyard character, but he has a clear enough eye for his own faults:

> '... even me and Jinnet hae a cast-oot noo and then. I'm aye the mair angry if I ken I'm wrang, and I've seen me that bleezin' bad-tempered that I couldna light my pipe, and we wadna speak to ane anither for oors and oors.'

And Johnnie Stark the Razor King, of *No mean city*, has his moment of introspection:

> 'There wis a time once... when Ah had an idea we should try to *be* something, Lizzie an' me... Ah can fight... but it seems Ah can do damn aw else.'

But the inferior examples in both schools share the same hallmark: a lack of effort, a contentment in serving up stock characters with stock responses, whether to love, death and the Kirk in the kailyard, or to violence and lust in gangland.

However, it is perhaps unfair to judge their writers by too high a standard. *Mutatis mutandis* we may say of their work what Edwin Muir said of the typical Scottish novel before World War I: 'It was sentimental, and it was written with one eye on the market'. These writers, notable for generally limited talent and frequent commercial success, are hardly due to be blamed for not carrying out a task which most of them can hardly have known to exist.

We have already hinted at some characteristics of the true Kailyard School of Scottish fiction, one being its rural setting in villages or small country towns. How can we justify the term 'urban kailyard'? The answer probably lies in those other qualities which mark out a kailyard novel, among them sentimentality and a certain smallness of vision, which flourish just as happily in a tenement close as in a cabbage patch. The 'reductive idiom' is recurrent in Scottish literature – a simplifying caricature, an attitude of 'who does he think he is?', or in the native tongue 'I kent his faither' – and the kailyard also deploys what may be called a 'comparative idiom'. The writer displays his characters, so pawky and quaint, with an air of amusement which he assumes his readers, comfortable in their own superiority, will share.

We may quote from the contents page of Roy's *Generalship*, even if this writer may be satirising the attitude rather than adopting it with approval.

Introduction – My Great Ambition – The Bath – The Bunker – The New House –
The Sideboard – John's Waistcoat and my Gown – Our Daughter Mary Ann – Lessons
in Music – Bailie Monro's Invitation – John's Terror and Surprise – Our New Piano.

The narrator's Great Ambition, it should be explained, is to have a house with a dining-room. Perhaps even more typical of the ethos of the kailyard is John's Terror when his daughter sits down at the piano, as far as he knows unable to play it, and shows every sign of 'affronting' him before Bailie Monro's guests. The Surprise is that Mary Ann, with her mother's connivance, has been taking piano lessons for six months. The whole minuscule episode well displays the kailyard viewpoint that domestic tragedies and triumphs, social gaffes and successes, are the most important things in life.

There is a final distinguishing mark of the kailyard, both rural and urban, which we have touched on earlier while remarking on its generally middle-class ambience: it is the high stockade of unshakeable assumptions within which the inhabitants of the kailyard live their untroubled lives.

In particular we may note that the hierarchy of society is most rigidly observed and respected. We have seen in *Generalship* the importance of not being affronted before a Bailie: 'Ye see,' it is explained, 'the Bailie's folk move in a circle, or maybe half a circle, aboon us.' Indeed this is one kailyard convention which persisted into what we shall be regarding as the era of the realistic novel. The son and daughter of Dot Allan's *The Deans* (1929), for instance, both marry 'out of their class'; the matches promise to be successful, but it is clearly thought (not least by the protagonists) rather extraordinary that this should be so. The situation of working-class girl and middle-class man (no uncommon theme, admittedly, in song and story) is delicately explored in John Macnair Reid's *Homeward journey* (1934) and more strongly in his *Judy from Crown Street*, which is set in 1933-4, though its date of composition is uncertain. And George Blake in *The shipbuilders* (1935) makes his riveter Danny Shields think of his boss, the shipyard owner, as 'a toff and a gentleman', and feel, in a night-club, 'an interloper on this territory proper to the toffs'.

Jeems Kaye, however, is not unduly concerned with class distinctions, though technically he probably does belong in the urban kailyard. He was the creation of Archibald Macmillan (the author's name was not given at the time, though we learn from Neil Munro's reminiscences *The brave days* that it was an open secret in Glasgow) and his letters on various subjects appeared in the Glasgow periodical *The Bailie* during the 1880s, being published soon after in book form. Jeems Kaye takes the keenest interest in contemporary affairs – we have his views on the 'Wet Review' of 1881 and the Egyptian war of 1882 – but many of his letters are on purely domestic topics, and correct behaviour, so important in the kailyard, looms large in his life. He is severely put out when a hen makes its way into church and ends up roosting on his head, a predicament with a fine flavour of the kailyard about it.

Probably the greatest interest for us lies in his observation of Glasgow life. He makes a memorable journey on the newly-opened underground railway (not the Subway, but what is now known as the low-level line from Queen Street), and his home area Stra'bungo fights its corner before the contemporary Boundary Commission, maintaining, like many small burghs in real life, that it should not be merged with the all-devouring city. His letter on 'The Caars' illustrates the fact, not only that the Glasgow public transport system is not what it used to be, but (to borrow a famous saying) that it never was. Jeems Kaye's 'caars' are horse-drawn tram-cars; he avoids using them whenever possible, comparing them unfavourably with 'oor auld tartan 'busses o' Menzies and McGregor'. He and his wife have to wait for a tram-car one cold night, and some of their experiences have a timeless quality:

> The first siven that came up were gaun tae the Goosedubs, and that, I need hardly say, was no oor road.

Nearly contemporary with *Jeems Kaye*, and also appearing originally in serial form (in another Glasgow weekly periodical, *Quiz*) is *Martha Spreull: being chapters in the life of a single wumman* (1884). We have looked at Martha earlier, as she evinces nostalgia for the slums of the Bell o' the Brae, and it is interesting to note that her author, though appearing as 'Zachary Fleming, writer', was the author of a number of purely kailyard works under his own name of Henry Johnston. (An elaborate pretence is made that the sketches are written by Martha herself and edited by her old friend Zachary Fleming, whom eventually she marries in a true kailyard happy ending.)

In spite of its tremendous coyness, comic mis-spellings, and heavy humour, there is a certain freshness about *Martha Spreull*. Martha writes as she speaks, in an easy Scots, and her view of Glasgow holds considerable interest for us. The setting is 1870 (since we find Glasgow University moving from High Street to Gilmorehill) so that we may estimate a date of about 1830 for Martha's childhood attack of the 'chincough' (whooping-cough). She was then taken 'doon to the waterside at Govan' for a change of air, where she sat on the grass picking buttercups and listening to the peaceful sound of shuttle and loom.

Erchie, the loquacious hero of *Erchie, my droll friend* by 'Hugh Foulis' (Neil Munro's pseudonym for his *Glasgow Evening News* sketches), is also inclined to look back, though perhaps in a more down-to-earth vein. His reminiscences appeared in book form in 1904, and we learn that he has been married 'four-and-forty year', so that his early married days are roughly contemporary with Martha Spreull's spinsterhood. Munro was, of course, a skilful journalist, and in *Erchie* he captures the very tone of the urban kailyard, couthy and contented, with a sharp eye for the customs and curiosities of its own small world. If not quite free of kailyard sentimentality, he generally steers clear of it in his sharp observation of city life. We are now in the city of the Glasgow Boys, and the admirer of Charles Rennie Mackintosh must treasure Erchie's detailed description of the Room de Luxe in the Willow Tearooms:

> ... The chairs is no' like ony ither chairs ever I clapped eyes on, but ye could easy guess they were chairs...

Erchie, like Martha Spreull, lives in a tenement, decidedly not the same thing as a slum, and the image of tenement life here is the traditionally couthy one. A clearer view was by now overdue, but was not to appear for another twenty years.

Such a view was certainly not supplied by J. J. Bell. He is perhaps the central figure of the urban kailyard, even though, of his many books, only some half-dozen are definitely set in Glasgow, and of these only one can be said to have attained lasting fame.

That one book, however, is *Wee Macgreegor*, an unpretentious collection of sketches about the small son of a working-class family, which was immensely popular from its first appearance in 1902. It had been rejected by several publishers on the grounds that its appeal was too local, and was originally published at Bell's own expense. It appeared on 23rd November; after one week the first printing was sold out, and by the end of the year sales totalled 20,000 copies.

It is now a minor classic, seldom out of print, with new editions from time to time; these often include sketches from both the original *Wee Macgreegor* and its first sequel, *Wee Macgreegor again* (1904). (The later sequels, *Courtin' Christina* and *Wee Macgreegor enlists*, have not survived in favour; Macgreegor by their time is a clean-cut and honourable youth, and his charm seems to have departed.) *Wee Macgreegor* has tended to baffle critics, who have severally regarded it as a simple, sentimental product of the kailyard (George Blake); a classic of Scottish humour (C. M. Grieve); and a social document (sociologist J. A. Mack). This very debate may indicate a certain depth under its good-humoured surface, which in turn may give us some clue to its contemporary popularity and present-day survival.

Quite forgotten, in contrast, is R. W. Campbell's Spud Tamson, once a Glasgow household word to rival the name of Macgreegor. He appeared first in 1915 in *Private Spud Tamson*, a strange mixture of comedy and heroics. Having enlisted in a moment of enthusiasm in 'the Glesca Mileeshy', and endured the ordeal of an army medical (his last bath having been at the previous Glasgow Fair), he ends up with sergeant's stripes, a bayonet wound and the Victoria Cross, before marrying his Gallowgate sweetheart Mary Ann:

> The whole Empire cried 'Well done', and all the world wondered at this hero from the slums.

He makes a fitting reappearance in *Sergt. Spud Tamson, V. C.* (1918), emigrates to join the Mounties in *Spud Tamson out west* (1924), and returns to help the mining village of Auchagree in its time of trouble in *Spud Tamson's pit* (1926). All of this is observed by the author, an army officer, with the tolerant superiority which we have already described, and enjoyed by, it can hardly be doubted, the middle-class reading public which contributed to the kailyard vogue.

So far, apart from a brief and questionably authentic glimpse of Spud Tamson's Gallowgate, our urban kailyard novel has had for its setting the tenement homes of the respectable working class, the urban equivalent, perhaps, of the small farmers, artisans and weavers who inhabit the rural kailyard. We should now consider briefly three novelists who take middle-class suburbia as the background of their books. A certain seriousness of intention further leads us to question whether they are really to be classed as kailyard authors, though kailyard elements are there. They are Annie S. Swan, O. Douglas and Mary Cleland, of whom the first two at least enjoyed considerable popularity, particularly with women readers, over a period of years spanning the two World Wars.

Annie S. Swan is not, of course, strictly a Glasgow novelist; some of her many books have suburban settings, but the majority take place in a somewhat standardised rural or small-town milieu. She figures in few histories of literature, but her writing, in book or serial form, reached a very large proportion of Scottish homes between 1883 (when her first novel *Aldersyde* was published) and her death in 1943. Enthusiasm for her work in some quarters is counterbalanced in others by profound distaste. Certainly no final judgment should be made without reference to her autobiography, which describes the alarmed reaction of her faithful public to her attempt at a 'serious' novel. It may be fair to say that, if limited in vision and talent, she was sincere in the use she made of what gifts she had; and this sincerity, recognised by her readers, may be at the root of her almost perennial popularity.

'O. Douglas' (Anna Buchan, sister of John) lived in Glasgow for some time when her father was minister of a South Side church. Most of her novels are set in the Borders countryside where she spent most of her life, but the two which can be classed as Glasgow novels, *The Setons* (1917) and *Eliza for common* (1928), have the South Side manse as background. They are gentle family stories, pleasant reading, appearing slightly out of their time beside the realistic, not to say pessimistic, contemporary 'Glasgow school'. O. Douglas, particularly in her earlier books, has a sharp enough eye for the foibles of middle-class suburbia, but the lasting impression of her art is of something sincere but slight, limited by the kailyard quality of contentment with the near view and the status quo.

The two windows (1922) and *The sure traveller* (1923) by 'Mary Cleland' (Margot Wells, another daughter of the manse) are interesting in their attempt to bring together the same middle-class suburbia and the near-slum tenement life which in reality (as John Cockburn saw) is often its neighbour. These are parallel novels, the first being the story of the waif Molly and the second that of the middle-class girl who befriends her. The setting is the 1890s; the theme – family disapproval of Catherine's longing to go to Girton – is promising and its development thoughtfully taken up; but the books are so gentle in tone as to have a certain uniformity. In Mary Cleland's novels as in those of O. Douglas, suburbia remains slightly dull.

For many years, we may remark, it consistently failed to come to life in Glasgow fiction. Few middle-class novels, until very lately, showed the qualities of power and passion found in the proletarian Glasgow novel at its best. If writers have avoided middle-class settings because they genuinely thought these had no potential for dramatic events, we may wonder whether some of the fault belongs to the urban kailyard, which has proved a remarkably tenacious genre.

It would be broadly correct to state that World War I marked the end of the Kailyard proper. The Glasgow novel of the 'twenties, as already noted, does begin to turn to social and political concerns; yet we have seen that the adventures of Spud Tamson continued well into that decade and that O. Douglas's *Eliza for common* appeared as late as 1928. Twenty years after *Wee Macgreegor*, J. J. Bell was still writing kailyard both rural and urban; his contributions to Glasgow fiction of the 'twenties are *The nickums* (1923) and *The braw bailie* (1925), which recognise the effects of neither war nor depression on their pawky little world.

We should not therefore leave the urban kailyard without considering *The McFlannels*. This amiable tenement family made its appearance during the 1940s in a series of BBC radio plays or sketches, and later in book form (five volumes, 1947-51). The main characters and their catch-phrases may still be recalled by elderly listeners today. Of these, Sarah's affronted 'Wullie, don't be vulgar!' encapsulates perfectly the kailyard tone, and marks *The McFlannels* as purest urban kailyard, surviving long after the heyday of the Kailyard School or even its recognised urban variants.

Special conditions may have favoured *The McFlannels*: production on radio, for instance, before television provided a wider choice of entertainment, or the wartime mood when, perhaps, the uncertainty of real life drew audiences towards the perceived security of the kailyard. Yet in more recent years such essentially kailyard productions as *Dr Finlay's casebook* and *[Take the] High road* have had high viewing figures, while steady sales have continued for periodicals like *The Sunday Post*, *People's Friend* and *The Scots Magazine*, homes of genuine kailyard stories (and attitudes). Scots do seem to be happy in the kailyard. Though for some years now the Glasgow novel has been in a realistic phase, some of the very latest items in this bibliography, published in the ironic 'nineties, are as couthy as can be, strengthening the possibility that the urban kailyard genre is not yet completely dead.

Neither is the Glasgow gang novel. Ron McKay's *Mean city* (1995) is one of the most recent (and most obvious) examples of the school. But this genre did not spring fully formed from the Gorbals soil in 1935 in the shape of *No mean city*: as early as 1923 there was a forerunner, George Blake's first novel *Mince Collop Close*.

This extraordinary mixture of melodrama and broad comedy is no less amazing, when viewed from this point in time, because we know of Blake's later 'Garvel' novels, those solid, and again rather dull, evocations of middle-class life. The heroine of *Mince Collop Close*, Bella Macfadyen, Queen of the Fan-Tans, is a figure of adolescent romance, a tall, handsome, slum-bred girl with flaming red-gold hair, attended by a faithful henchman and dowered with superhuman ingenuity, self-confidence and luck. After the opening chapters, which describe Bella's childhood and rise to power as a gang-leader, the book falls away into a series of disconnected episodes, reminding us that, though Blake was thirty years old and an experienced journalist when it was published, *Mince Collop Close* is the work of an inexperienced novelist.

It is not entirely without merit. It is an early essay in realism, pre-dated in its depiction of slums mainly by the Victorian tracts and the works of Patrick MacGill, and Blake reproduces honestly enough, here and there with the simplicity of good writing, the reality of life in the Cowcaddens slums. The urge to escape from such a life is one reason put forward, in the famous *No mean city* and elsewhere, for the rise of the Glasgow gangs.

No mean city was published under the names of Alexander McArthur and H. Kingsley Long. The publishers' preface to the first edition sets out the arrangement whereby Long, a journalist, organised McArthur's striking but poorly presented manuscripts. One would not expect a literary masterpiece to emerge in this way, and indeed *No mean city* is loosely constructed and clumsily written. Nevertheless it became, and has remained, the Glasgow novel best known (at least by title) to the general public, and at the time of writing, more than sixty years after its first publication, it is still available in paperback.

Its fame, or notoriety, may be reasonably attributed to the immediate, and to some extent continuing, objections to its depiction of the Gorbals. Slums and violence had by 1935 already been bracketed together in Glasgow novels, but seldom at such length or in such colourful detail. Whether such descriptions are purely sensational or factual reportage is perhaps for the sociologist to decide; given the book's joint authorship, it seems reasonable to suppose that there is a little of both. A desire to expose the intolerable living conditions seems to lie behind the writing of *No mean city*, and there are many small touches of social description which do have an air of truthful reporting, as well as an attempt to explain the pressures which lead to violence and a suggestion that there is potential for better things even in a Razor King. However unskilfully handled, these elements are perhaps sufficient to set *No mean city* apart from the brood of inferior imitations which followed it.

It is not uncommon for a best-seller to start a vogue, but *No mean city* has cast a particularly long shadow over the Glasgow novel. If the name of *No bad money* (1969) seems familiar, that is because this rather undistinguished novel was compiled from fragmentary papers of McArthur's long after his death in 1947, with the addition of considerable new material by a different collaborator, Peter Watts, and a title calculated to remind the bookstall browser of the famous original. From John McNeillie's *Glasgow keelie* (1940) to the 1995 novel by Ron McKay already cited, by way of Bill McGhee's *Cut and run* (1962) which evokes *No mean city* on its paperback cover as a sort of passport to success, the bandwagon rolled on for many years.

In recent Glasgow fiction, however, the gangs seem to have slipped into place, no longer some unthinkably sinister threat but part of a larger crime scene; a scene which contains drugs, money-lenders, and violence so pervasive that, ironically, the traditional gangs are viewed in a positively urban-kailyard light. Where they do appear, new approaches are found. William McIlvanney's *Laidlaw* (1977) depicts an underworld before whose grim professionalism the gang boys back down. In George Friel's *Mr Alfred M. A.* (1972), the pervasive graffiti of rival gangs helps to build up the nightmarish cityscape of the closing scenes. A sequence of stories in Alan Spence's *Its colours they are fine* (1977) traces almost casually, with enormous effect, the development, or degeneration, of a street-wise small boy to become a hard man with a steel comb in his pocket. There is no overt blame or excuse for Shuggie, but understanding is there. Any serious Glasgow gang novel which may appear will have to take its place in the corpus of realistic fiction about Glasgow.

5   The Realistic Glasgow Novel

Glasgow fiction, like Scottish fiction as a whole, took a new direction after the First World War. We see a concern for realism; an attempt to make some statement about human life and relationship without lapsing into sentimentality on the one hand or melodrama on the other. There have been three distinct 'waves' of Glasgow fiction, each with its own particular character or preoccupation.

They are 'the Glasgow school' of the 'twenties, the first substantial body of non-kailyard fiction about Glasgow; the 'proletarian' wave of the 'thirties, greatly concerned with the contemporary problems of politics, depression and unemployment; and what has been called, in earlier editions of this bibliography, 'the post-war wave'. We shall look at each in turn. The post-war wave, however, reached new heights in the early nineteen-seventies, to the extent that the novels of the last three decades demand to be treated in a section of their own.

The 'twenties

By the end of World War I, as we have seen, the main impetus of the kailyard movement was spent. The ground had been prepared for the realistic novel by two works of genius, George Douglas Brown's *The house with the green shutters* (1901) and John MacDougall Hay's *Gillespie* (1914). They are the antithesis of kailyard fiction, realistic to the point of grimness, all the more effective because they are set in rural communities comparable to the idyllic parishes of the kailyard writers.

The house with the green shutters in particular has, because of the mirror-image of the kailyard which it seems to present, at times been regarded as essentially a counterblast to this movement. But it has also been argued that the novel has too much power to be simply a move in a literary debate, and that Brown's quarrel was not merely with the writers who were failing to observe the contemporary scene with any clarity, but with the scene itself in its ugliness and distortion of values.

The writers in the first wave of Glasgow novels, far behind Brown as most of them are in ability and vision, seem to have this direct rather than literary motivation. They consistently declare against the kailyard virtues of contentment, sobriety, fidelity and conservatism, but not for the sake of rejecting the kailyard; there is no explicit recognition of such a school. Rather it is that they have observed the contemporary world with dissatisfaction and see no reason to accept the status quo. However tentatively to begin with – several of them went on to write much better novels – they are coming to grips with contemporary Glasgow.

The first of this group to appear, Catherine Carswell's *Open the door!* (1920), is the only Glasgow novel of the 'twenties to have survived in critical esteem, having fallen out of

Catherine Carswell
Scottish Book Collector, v. 2 no. 6
August/September 1990

Dot Allan
R.D. MacLeod ed., *Modern Scottish Literature,* 1933

George Blake
Scotland's Magazine, November 1959

Neil Munro
D. Walker Brown, *Clydeside Litterateurs,* 1897

sight for a long time but being rediscovered in recent years. An exception among its contemporaries in other ways, it is a strikingly original work for its time, and remarkably little dated in its sensitive insight into a woman's feelings. The setting of its early episodes is Edwardian middle-class West End Glasgow, evoking well that pleasant time and place. Joanna escapes from her Calvinistic girlhood – that very home background so treasured by the kailyarders – into an early brief marriage to a possessive Italian, followed by a long and chequered affair with a married painter. With extreme honesty Carswell (who admired and was encouraged by D. H. Lawrence) traces Joanna's childhood stirrings of sensuality, the idyll of her first love, her passionate awakening in marriage, and the stormy emotions of her young womanhood. The coy reticence of the kailyard might never have existed, near though it is in time to *Open the door!*

Carswell's second novel, *The camomile* (1922), is in epistolary form and at first glance seems a lighter work, though with a similar theme. The period and setting are the same (Joanna from *Open the door!* appears briefly as a minor character). Ellen, back from studying music in Germany, chafes against the Calvinistic background of her aunt's house, and takes a room (a daring move, it is made clear) where she can go at times to work. But the work she wants to do is writing, and *The camomile* is a cool examination of the situation of the woman writer in that place and at that time.

Dot Allan also considers this question in *Makeshift* (1928). Most of her novels are conscientious and thoughtful essays in Glasgow realism, lacking only a certain creative spark which might have given them a rather higher place in the hierarchy of the Glasgow novel. *The syrens* (1921) is honest but pedestrian, the story of a young man who works his way to success in the grocery trade but eventually succumbs to the wanderlust inherited from his sailor father. *The Deans* (1929) sets out to be a realistic tenement story, but Allan is not at home in this specific milieu, though her knowledge of and affection for Glasgow in general is clearly seen. She reaches a higher level of understanding and writing in *Hunger march* (1934), which we shall consider in its chronological place, and in the almost completely forgotten *Makeshift*.

In the opening pages of *Makeshift* the heroine's mother commits suicide, having said to her uncomprehending small daughter:

'Second best… That's what my life has been made up of, Jacqueline; makeshift all the time.'

The main part of the book is a sensitively observed account of Jacqueline's girlhood and growing up, as she leaves home to work in Glasgow and experiences both loneliness and love. She accepts a proposal of marriage largely in order to escape the dreaded fate – as it was then seen – of the 'surplus woman' , compassionately presented by Allan. She doesn't love the young man, and what is worse, he doesn't understand her urge and need to write; this is what persuades her to take the train to London, determined that her life at least will not be 'makeshift'. Dot Allan here achieves a thoughtful novel which should be better known.

George Blake was still searching for his true voice. *The wild men* (1925) is less melodramatic than his debut novel *Mince Collop Close*, though as a story of Glasgow Bolsheviks it is not yet a depiction of the everyday city. In *Young Malcolm* (1926) he seems at first to regress alarmingly towards the kailyard, with a slightly priggish and lachrymose hero who graduates with high distinction as a doctor and marries his sweetheart to rescue her from a drunken father and uncongenial stepmother. Yet there is a streak of toughness in Malcolm, who carries on his research, refusing the offer of a well-paid but humdrum general practice, until the arrival of a baby, credibly enough, makes student life impossible. Blake does not succumb to the kailyard lure of a happy ending, and the many-sided Glasgow scene is sharply observed.

So far the spectrum of the realistic Glasgow novel, though stretching from Cowcaddens slums to West End terraces, had lacked a story of ordinary people living in the typical Glasgow tenement, and this lack John Cockburn set out to supply in *Tenement* (1925). It is probably not too unfair to phrase it thus, for the book reads very much as if it had been written to order, and the long 'Apology' or preface in essay form reinforces this impression. It is an accurate enough portrayal of tenement life, if leaning towards the dark side of the cosy urban kailyard picture; but Cockburn, judging by his preface, appears convinced of the total dullness of his subject, and unfortunately he convinces the reader too.

The Glasgow novels of the 'twenties (with the exception, as we have remarked, of Catherine Carswell's work) have not survived to the present day in either popular favour or critical esteem. They form, as it were, a first draft of the realistic Glasgow novel. We must give these writers credit for leaving the kailyard behind and setting out in a new direction, but their main service was in opening the way for some rather more important work in the next few years.

The 'thirties

A chronological list of Glasgow novels, such as that accompanying this bibliography, shows clearly the sudden quantitative increase in this decade. Closer inspection reveals the salient point of the novels of the 'thirties: their political and social commitment. Quite forgotten is the kailyard acceptance of 'the poor' as a fact of life, the kailyard recognition of hierarchy and establishment. The 'proletarian' novel, to use a term popularised by George Blake among others, is the typical one of this decade.

Several distinct themes are evident. We may isolate first two novels linked by their treatment of politics, in the sense of electioneering and the hustings, though both are primarily interested in rather larger concerns: Robert Craig's *O people!* (1932) and Catherine Gavin's *Clyde valley* (1938).

Craig's novel is a strange mixture of realism and romantic patriotism. The hero is a solitary idealist obsessed with the desire to see Scotland a full member of the League of Nations: his visionary eloquence is diverted to help the Socialist cause at a by-election. The extended passages of rhyming prose which glorify a romantic image of Scotland contrast oddly with the accurate and humorous rendering of heckling at political meetings.

The view of the hustings in *Clyde valley* is less sympathetic. The young central character is involved in them because of her love-affair with the candidate, an unhappily married man, and finds the proceedings unbearably sordid, with a relentless insistence on sectarianism and on her own part in the candidate's life. The novel is unevenly written, but a powerful effect of frustrated passion remains with the reader, stemming both from the heroine's doomed love and from her relationship with her mother, who harbours a strange repressed jealousy of her.

These novels, like so many of the period, touch on the slums. It may be unfair to suggest that this was almost obligatory in the Glasgow novel of the 'thirties; many of the descriptions are striking enough, but in a journalistic way, as if the writers lack the ability to convey exactly what they have seen and felt. Fortunately in this decade two Scottish writers of the first rank, Neil Gunn and Edwin Muir, turned their attention to Glasgow and its slums. Their Glasgow novels are not the works nearest their hearts, but both convey with great conviction the almost physical effect of the slums on sensitive observers.

Gunn's novel *Wild geese overhead* (1939) contrasts city and country life simply enough: a young newspaperman takes lodgings outside the city, and so experiences daily the peace and beauty of one way of life after the racket and ugliness of the other. Yet the city of his newspaper office is different again from the one he discovers in the slums:

> ...the feeling of unease, of half-nightmare. And the smell, the pervasive smell that dried up the back of the nostrils, held something more than squalor, something vaguely threatening. The whole body went on the defensive, sensitive to the atmosphere, as the ear-drum to a threatened sound.

Edwin Muir's *Poor Tom* (1932) is of particular interest because of its strong element of autobiography. The family situation in the novel is almost exactly similar to that in Muir's own life, and at least one passage in his *An autobiography* of 1954, describing Muir's sense of oppression in walking along Eglinton Street, parallels the words of the narrator in *Poor Tom*. Clearly Muir is inspired by personal experience and conviction in his description of Glasgow; and while its weighting with fact means that the novel struggles to take on a full life of its own, this poet's impression of the slums adds welcome depth to an otherwise rather prosaic picture.

In our concern for slum Glasgow, we should not forget that middle-class Glasgow still existed, even in the proletarian 'thirties, and that it was used as background by a few writers of the decade. Frederick Niven, for instance, continued to write during the nineteen-twenties and 'thirties, and his Glasgow novels give a good impression of mercantile and middle-class life from about 1890 to the outbreak of World War I. They are to some extent parallel novels, since a character from one book may often be mentioned, in passing, in another. *A tale that is told* (1920) is a leisurely, gentle, perceptive account of large and small events in the narrator's family; *The three Marys* (1930) is again a story of a Glasgow artist, a few years on in time from *Justice of the peace*; in *The rich wife* (1932) a Glasgow woman returns as on a pilgrimage to the South Side flat which was her childhood home.

Worth closer consideration are *Mrs Barry* (1933) and *The staff at Simson's* (1937). Mrs Barry is a widow struggling against illness and financial problems on behalf of her small son Neil. They live in a poor district of Glasgow, though not in the slums. The story is undramatic and sometimes moving; among its best features is Neil's view of their 'shipbuilding parish', significant details selected with a painter's eye.

If *Mrs Barry* is the character study of one woman, *The staff at Simson's* is a group portrait. This is Niven's full treatment of the Glasgow warehouse life so effectively sketched twenty-three years before in *Justice of the peace.* Unlike the Moirs in the earlier book, individual characters are not here treated in depth, but are quickly and deftly delineated: the period, just as before, is about 1890-1910, and each member of the 1890 staff is accompanied, in near-documentary style, through the major events of his life. The main concern, however, is the picture of Glasgow business life and the to-and-fro of a textile warehouse, and this is excellently done. Niven was for a short time an apprentice in such a firm, and clearly youthful memories play a part in *The staff at Simson's*.

Niven may not, in the final analysis, be a novelist of the first rank – there are occasional longeurs and awkward patches in even his best books – but the intensity of vision and feeling with which he recalled the Glasgow of his youth has been transferred to his novels, and must give him a high place among Glasgow novelists.

The place of George Woden is less certain. A prolific author over some forty years, he wrote a number of light detective and romantic novels, several readable if rather pedestrian novels with a middle-class background, and one genuine contribution to Glasgow fiction, *Mungo* (1932). It is a family story covering the period 1890-1930, and like *Wax fruit* and *Justice of the peace* deals with a Glasgow businessman. We see young John Mungo and Mary Bell running away to Glasgow to make their fortune: we follow their early happiness and struggles, seeing them in a bad patch at the turn of the century and in modest prosperity a few years later, and return to them in middle age, with a grown-up family, enjoying their hard-earned wealth. While not a particularly dramatic story, it is notably human and well-balanced, recognising John's solid common sense and kindness as well as his *nouveau riche* fancies.

John Macnair Reid carried out in two novels the delicate feat of placing working-class and middle-class Glasgow side by side. *Homeward journey* (1934) is a first novel, with some evidence of immaturity in the writing and the heart-searching of the young hero, but it is an honest attempt at depicting the class distinctions of contemporary Glasgow, through the love affair of a middle-class boy and a girl from a slum home. The affair is insecurely based – the boy wants to escape from the memory of his dominating mother and the girl is ambitious for social advancement – and the lovers return to their own circles with a feeling almost of relief. In Reid's posthumously published *Judy from Crown Street* (1970) the situation is comparable, but the lovers are older and there is a happy ending, if rather glibly brought about. The Gorbals-Pollokshields gulf is still seen as an immutable fact of life (which betrays perhaps the date of composition, obviously before Reid's premature death in 1954), but there is a certain maturity in the characterisation: Judy is finely presented, warm, down-to-earth and human, and Grannie, with whom she lives, a tough, humorous and credible old battleaxe.

If we were to select the major Glasgow novel of the 'thirties, however, the choice might lie among four books published in the middle years of the decade: Dot Allan's *Hunger march* (1934), George Blake's *The shipbuilders* (1935), James Barke's *Major operation* (1936) and Edward Shiels's *Gael over Glasgow* (1937). They share a similar setting, Clydeside during the depression (shipbuilding Clydeside, in the last three cases), and the social problem of unemployment, particularly its enervating effect, is the unifying theme.

The novels by Allan and Shiels are comparatively little known. *Hunger march* is technically adroit, its action confined to twenty-four hours in an unnamed but recognisable Glasgow on the day of a hunger march, one of many in the depression years. We focus in turn on a merchant whose business is in trouble; on his cleaner and her long-term unemployed son; on a charismatic revolutionary who wants to change the system, and on a young middle-class radical trying to make sense of it all. There is a clear 'two cities' theme and Allan overtly condemns the uncaring middle class, while giving full value to the despair of the businessman and his sense of responsibility towards his workers. It is a balanced and thoughtful view.

The hero of *Gael over Glasgow* is a young Clydebank-Irish engineer with a constant dream (due to his Gaelic heritage) of leaving the city for a new life in the Highlands. The writing is sensitive and honest, with genuine feeling for the boy's growing up and the effect of unemployment and strike action on his idealism and sense of responsibility. Some of the shipyard scenes attain a pitch of fierce beauty. The fairy-tale ending (in which a rich uncle makes the boy's dream come true) is disappointing after the unsensational realism of the book so far, but there is a humanly understandable reason for this, linked to the autobiographical element which the reader may have suspected. Edward Shiels was himself an engineer in Clydebank and a keen country walker in his youth; he contracted polio in his twenties and was confined to a wheelchair until his early death. The wish-fulfilment ending of his novel, it can hardly be doubted, stems from these circumstances.

The Barke and Blake novels were greatly praised in their time and have been the subject of critical consideration again in recent years. *Major operation*, still one of the most impressive urban-proletarian novels, is a fine book with memorable passages of angry description deliberately inset in the action of the story. The bourgeois Anderson and the workers' leader Jock MacKelvie are brought side by side in a hospital ward, each awaiting an operation, and thus their diverging points of view can be presented and argued over, sometimes at rather implausible length. MacKelvie is a strong, well-realised character, and his sincerity is beyond doubt, but when – in a hospital ward – he speaks for five or six pages on Materialism, love, or the workers' movement, he taxes our belief.

Anderson, the businessman, is rather less real throughout, and credibility fails when he throws in his lot with the working-class and dies heroically saving MacKelvie from the hooves of a police horse. Our final impression of *Major operation* may be that it is rather overweighted by its political content, but in this very concentration on politics and concern for the workers it is a book of its time, and a high point in the succession of Glasgow proletarian novels.

George Blake, who had begun to turn his attention to middle-class life in 'Garvel' (Greenock), returned to Glasgow settings for two depression novels. *David and Joanna* (1936) is the oddly idyllic story of a boy and girl who meet through an interest in cycling – more exactly, through the need to escape from the depression-hit city – and spend the summer in a tent in a Highland glen. Though (as in *Young Malcolm*) the idyll, realistically, has to end, it is implied that they will take up the good life again.

But Blake's *The shipbuilders* (1935) was his major attempt at depicting Glasgow in the depression, and in some ways is a near approach to the complete Glasgow novel. It traces the effect of the depression on two men: Leslie Pagan, a shipyard owner, and Danny Shields, a riveter in the yard (and Pagan's batman during World War I). It is their relationship which must seem problematic today, patronising as it is on Pagan's side and uncritically devoted on Danny's; the reader may further have reservations about Danny's general attitude of deference to all 'toffs' and ex-officers, and Pagan's habit of dropping in to O'Glinchey's public house to drink with the 'rough innocents' from his yard. Blake himself seems in later years to have recognised some falseness in the tone of the book, thinking it 'unworthy of its epic subject.'

But we have already noted his journalist's eye for detail, and in *The shipbuilders* he selects scene after scene, building up a full and sympathetic picture of Glasgow and of the plight of the unemployed. There is a classic description of a Rangers-Celtic football match; a journey down the Clyde past the many shipyards lying idle; a sequence in the High Court as Danny's son stands trial for murder; and frequently we come back to Danny, walking the city in his idleness,

> discovering queer, quiet streets… that told him a doleful story of the city's vastness and complexity and indifference.

The shipbuilders shows a certain unevenness of characterisation; critics differ quite drastically on whether the middle-class or the working-class household is the more convincing, and perhaps the answer is that both are to some extent stereotyped and hence ring untrue. The class-consciousness already mentioned runs through the book, impossible for a modern reader to ignore. It is therefore a flawed novel, but in an overall view of the decade it stands out as an honest attempt to depict the whole of Glasgow, however impossible that has proved to be. In *The shipbuilders* we can see what Glasgow writers of the 'thirties are trying to do.

The post-war wave
Just as notable as the 'wave' of Glasgow fiction in the nineteen-thirties is the remarkable

increase in both the quantity and the quality of Glasgow novels published in the twenty-five years after the end of World War II. Not all are masterpieces, and greater things were to follow from the 'seventies onwards, but this period was at least a seed-bed, and indeed a time in which we can at last confidently speak of good Glasgow novels, in terms of their content, originality and technical expertise.

While the typical post-war Glasgow novel is an examination of contemporary society, some writers still look back in anger or in nostalgia. This process has produced some of the finest writing we have yet been able to consider, in Edward Gaitens's *Dance of the apprentices* (1948) and John J. Lavin's *Compass of youth* (1953), both set during the early years of the twentieth century.

Dance of the apprentices is in part an expansion of some of the short stories in Gaitens's earlier collection *Growing up* (1942), and it may be that Gaitens's real genius was for the short story form. Since *Growing up* has long been out of print, however, his work is more readily judged by *Dance of the apprentices*, which is (predictably perhaps) episodic in structure, with a rather awkward time-lapse at the end of book 1, but yet contains some of the most authentic, thoughtful and skilfully-written Glasgow scenes in fiction to this date. The chapters, or stories, have the air of being sketches from life, observed in the sharpest detail, with humour and understanding. The thread linking the episodes is the story of young Eddy Macdonnel and his friends, the apprentices of the title, as they grow up, court their girl-friends, discover politics, philosophy and literature, and choose prison as conscientious objectors at the outbreak of World War I. Book 2 looks forward some fifteen years to find them in the 'world fit for heroes' to which they have returned.

Compass of youth is also the story of a boy growing up in the years before World War I, and again has no really developed plot. Its great strength is in evocation of the sights, and especially the sounds, of 'The Square', the East End block of tenements. In spite of a probable autobiographical content, the novel preserves a fine detachment in observing the neighbours in 'The Square': the eccentric 'Professor' and the clairvoyant Mrs Young modulate from figures of fun to human beings whose stories are told with considerable understanding and compassion. Continually passing across the vision of the sensitive young narrator are two figures of tragedy, Rab Young, the golden football hero blinded in a mine disaster, and Rachel McAllister, once his girl-friend and now a prostitute. In the chapter describing their last meeting, Lavin's writing, always accurate and considered, reaches an unexpected pitch of power and controlled emotion.

A second group of post-war novelists looks back to the Glasgow of the nineteen-thirties already so thoroughly charted by contemporary writers. J. F. Hendry in *Fernie brae* (1947) provides an impressionistic, child's-eye view of tenement, school and university life between the wars. Again this has the air of a piece of autobiography in fictional form, sensitively written but perhaps short of emotional power.

In contrast, David Lambert's two novels about Clydeside workers, *He must so live* (1956) and *No time for sleeping* (1958), are inferior in literary quality but infused with political and social concern. They are set in the nineteen-thirties, and, though in fact published much later, have a strong affinity to the political-proletarian novels of that decade. The story of one family is carried through the two books, but the main setting is 'the Yard foundry', and the main protagonists the men who work there, involved in the intricate politics of the factory, the town, and eventually the country, when a delegation is sent to London to demand that 'Chamberlain must go'.

Hugh Munro's *The Clydesiders* (1961) covers a period from the late nineteen-twenties to the early war years, showing the effect of the depression on one family. It is tempting (if only because of the similarity in titles) to draw a comparison with *The shipbuilders*, but this is a very different book. It is written from the working-class viewpoint, and it is a mark of the new school of Glasgow fiction that this can at last be achieved without either self-consciousness or a chip on the shoulder. (Munro's later *The keelie* (1978) is the deeply felt story, again probably autobiographical, of a working-class Glasgow boy struggling to gain success as a writer.) The family in *The Clydesiders* includes an unemployed father striving to accept, with difficulty but without melodrama, his new position of 'unimportance' in the household. The mother, Julia, is a notably strong character, moral, unselfish and proud, but far from being the kailyard heroine this might suggest. She imposes high standards on her family calmly, relentlessly, but with a saving humour. The impression of tenement life is worlds away from that of the old slum-oriented Glasgow novel.

But the typical post-war author is writing about contemporary Glasgow, and doing so with a new insight and skill. Several writers first published in the late 'sixties (like George Friel and William McIlvanney) reached new heights as Glasgow fiction gathered strength after 1970, and are best considered in a later chapter. Meanwhile a new school of Glasgow writers was looking at the city with fresh eyes. A distinctly original view of adolescence is found in Clifford Hanley's *A taste of too much* (1960). Hanley's literary style is light and racy, and his characters tend to talk rather too much, but here he has produced a perceptive study of an adolescent boy, tracing school and family relationships with considerable understanding. On the surface the dialogue is a constant rattle of dry Glasgow humour, but the boy is seen to be searching for a different form of expression. His story gains point from its setting in a council housing scheme, seldom considered as a background for fiction.

Chaim Bermant's perceptive and funny picture of adolescence in *Jericho sleep alone* (1964) has a similarly fresh background in the Glasgow Jewish community, its warm predictability at first irritating to a boy in his last year at school but rather welcome after his experiences on a kibbutz. These are intelligent and articulate boys with stable home backgrounds; very different are the young toughs of Hugh C. Rae's *Night pillow* (1967). Such boys in Glasgow fiction hitherto have invariably been products of the slums. Rae makes the point that in the 'sixties they are just as likely to live in new blocks of flats, with every modern convenience but surrounded by soul-destroying bleakness and lack of human contact. The lives of three boys and of a hastily-married young middle-class couple come together with the inevitable quality of tragedy.

Old age has been less frequently dealt with in Glasgow fiction, but it has produced a small masterpiece in Robert Nicolson's *Mrs Ross* (1961), with its sequel *A flight of steps* (1966). Together they form the sympathetic, humorous and tender story of a lonely old woman, living in a condemned tenement, sustained by her dreams of an imaginary past, and thinking she is spied on by unseen watchers in the building. In the first novel she is rescued, cleaned up, restored to health and reunited with her husband, but by the second book this is a dimly remembered episode, and in the continuation of her story – with the added small tragedy that her real world, Shawl Street, is being pulled down around her – there can be no happy ending. Nicolson sees beyond the dirty, grotesque exterior and depicts in these two short books the essential old woman, independent, vulnerable and alive.

Archie Hind's *The dear green place* bore, on its first publication in 1966, the rather tepid description 'an autobiographical, documentary novel'. It has proved to be more significant than that would imply. Hind's description of Glasgow conveys both importance and atmosphere as successfully as any novel we have yet considered. The writing becomes convoluted and slightly awkward at times in the effort to convey the narrator's beliefs and philosophy, but when Hind turns to the description of something clearly observed he writes with economy, precision and beauty. The chapter set in the slaughterhouse has this directness, and as it happens Hind, in the person of the narrator Mat, says soon afterwards:

> Above all this [the slaughterhouse routine] there was something which Mat counted as important and which he had tried to formulate clearly to himself; it was the need to be intimately involved in a material process.

Hind is referring to urban man in general, but it does seem that concern for the material and actual brings immediacy and power to his writing.

The importance of *The dear green place*, viewed thirty years later, is that Mat is a working-class writer, struggling not just with his great work but with the perception that writing isn't for people like him. Though the novel ends in despair, it proved in reality to be not an end but a beginning. Glasgow writers were emboldened by *The dear green place*, and it has a claim to be considered seminal in the flowering of Glasgow fiction during the next two decades.

The long and distinguished writing career of Robin Jenkins, beginning in the 'fifties, has continued into the 'nineties, but we shall look here at three comparatively early novels, the most definably 'Glasgow' of his works. In *Guests of war* (1956) he chose a theme surprisingly little handled in Scottish fiction, the wartime evacuation of a city school to a small country town. 'Gowburgh' is readily identifiable as Glasgow and the school is a primary school from the slums. The reactions of guests and hosts and the further impact of the Gowburgh mothers – a tremendous gallery of portraits – are presented with insight and humour.

The outstanding figure in *Guests of war* is Bell McShelvie, one of these mothers. Yearning to return to her country childhood, she seizes the chance to accompany the children to

Alexander McArthur
Daily Record and Mail, 1 November 1935

Edward Gaitens
The Holiday Book, 1946

George Friel
Edinburgh Review, 71, 1985
Photo James Gillespie

Archie Hind
Glasgow Museums: The People's Palace. Reproduced with permission of Alasdair Gray, artist

Langrigg, though this means leaving her husband and remaining family in Gowburgh. Her conscience tells her that this desertion is wrong and will have to be atoned for. Tragedy indeed follows, and she accepts it like a tragic heroine, turning back to the dirty, despised, yet human and vulnerable city with a new understanding and dedication. Jenkins has a fine touch in depicting women, particularly those outwardly grotesque, middle-aged and shabby; Bell McShelvie is one of his best creations, and one of the strongest female characters in Scottish fiction.

In *The changeling* (1958) he juxtaposes the slums with the suburbs in the story of a bright Glasgow child, a petty thief from a miserable home, who is befriended by a middle-class schoolmaster and taken on a family holiday to the Firth of Clyde. Tom's reaction to normal family life, and the none too enthusiastic reaction of the teacher's children to Tom, form the first sequence of contrasts, but a much more violent confrontation follows when Tom's sluttish mother and her cronies seek out the family party. The ending is one of shock and despair, in which we are left to consider the complexity of human motives.

Jenkins's *A very Scotch affair* (1968) is in intention and effect a real Glasgow novel, the city no mere backcloth but an integral part of scene and action. The setting is east-end Bridgeton, called 'the ghetto' and seen as permanently marking its inhabitants with the stigma of social inferiority. Jenkins explores his characters pitilessly, in particular his hero – so to call him – Mungo Niven, who callously leaves his dying wife to go abroad with his mistress, returning after Bess's death to the execration of the ghetto women. Bess, the fat, loving wife whom Mungo has come to find unbearably irritating, is one of Jenkins's finest creations; Andrew, the coldly selfish son, is drawn with unsparing accuracy and very little sympathy. As for Niven, we move from seeing events through his eyes to seeing him through those of his horrified neighbours, and therefore we are left with questions in our minds. Can he be quite such a monster as they think him? Or can he possibly consider himself justified in his betrayal of Bess?

And not the least of our questions about this complex and disturbing book must be whether the 'ghetto' has really – as Mungo likes to imply – made him the man he is. It is in this sense that the city may be regarded as being, in a more subtle way than earlier writers have contrived, a prime mover in the action; and if we take this view, *A very Scotch affair* undoubtedly marks a high point in the story of the Glasgow novel.

6   Since 1970

While it is usual, and broadly correct, to name 1981 as an *annus mirabilis* in Glasgow fiction because of the publication of Alasdair Gray's *Lanark*, things were already happening in the 1970s. Above all, perhaps, this will come to be seen as the decade of George Friel. Though the publication of Friel's five novels spanned some sixteen years and a number of short stories had appeared earlier, his masterpiece *Mr Alfred M. A.* was published in 1972 and the less-known but equally brilliant *Grace and Miss Partridge* just before our target date, in 1969. Only in recent years has his writing begun to receive the critical attention it deserves.

Friel's first novel, *The bank of time* (1959), is a solid but not especially original debut, the story of the youngest of three brothers from boyhood through to first love. Strikingly different is *The boy who wanted peace* (1964). In the story of a gang of small boys who find (and worship) the money from a bank robbery – realistically improbable perhaps, but on a deeper level totally convincing – we find several features which will recur in Friel's work: the leading character as loner, self-consciously out of step with ordinary life; the world of school, observed and presented with deadly accuracy; and the beginnings of a Joycean word-play seldom seen in Scottish, let alone Glasgow, fiction.

To call *Grace and Miss Partridge* a tenement story, though superficially accurate, does less than justice to the subtlety and rich, adventurous language with which it explores the old woman's obsession with the little girl Grace, hinting at the events in Miss Partridge's past life which underlie her present lonely eccentricity. *Mr Alfred M. A.* traces the decline of a seedy middle-aged schoolmaster whose ill-advised affection for a young girl pupil hastens the process which his drinking has begun. Grim as the theme is, a detached, ironic quality in the writing carries the story with deceptive lightness towards a nightmarish sequence in which Mr Alfred meets a mysterious figure called Tod – the Devil, as aficionados of Scottish fiction will assume – and a climax of black humour.

After the power and precision of these two books, Friel's last novel *An empty house* (1975) makes a slighter impression, but has fine moments of atmospheric description: the broken-down old house in its tangled garden is perhaps (as the title suggests) the best-realised character of all.

We should mention here the interesting upsurge of the Glasgow short story since 1970: not so much the form itself, since that had been steadily growing in power for some decades (see *Streets of stone*, an anthology edited in 1985 by the present writer and Hamish Whyte), but its appearance in such collections as Alan Spence's *Its colours they are fine* (1977). Short story collections by Kelman, Gray, MacDougall and others will be found in this bibliography, testifying to the further growth of the genre in Glasgow. *Its colours they are fine* is in fact a story sequence, in an uncompromising rendering of Glasgow speech: unsentimental, precisely observed glimpses of childhood, adolescence and young manhood, each story shedding light on the others, building up a harsh, beautiful, three-dimensional picture of the various faces of Glasgow, tough, bigoted, humorous and tender. Nothing like it had previously been seen in Glasgow fiction.

The same might be said of Evelyn Cowan's *Portrait of Alice* (1976). Alice, fifty years old, comes home after a nervous breakdown, into much the same conditions (as we gradually learn) which triggered it, and grimly tries to rebuild her life. Her wealthy Jewish family and social circle are all too convincingly portrayed as Cowan, with considerable skill and control, handles the threads of Alice's experience, inevitably twining into another pattern of crisis. For a comparably strong and honest Glasgow novel by and about a woman, we must probably look back to *Open the door!*

Significant in another way was the publication of *The breadmakers* (1972), heralding the energetic writing career of Margaret Thomson Davis. *The breadmakers* and its sequels,

William McIlvanney
Scotland on Sunday 4 August 1991
Photo Adam Elder, courtesy of *Scotland on Sunday*

James Kelman
Glasgow Museums: The People's Palace. Reproduced with permission of Alasdair Gray, artist

Photograph of Alasdair Gray in unbuttoned mood.

Alasdair Gray
Books in Scotland 28, 1988
Reproduced with permisssion
of Alasdair Gray, artist

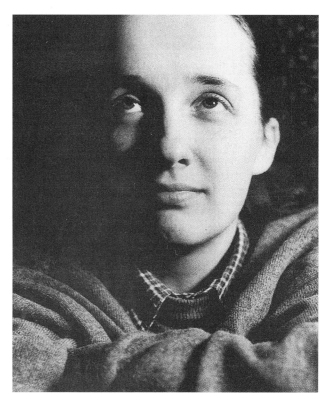

A.L. Kennedy
Scotsman 11 January 1997
Photo Stephen Mansfield

A baby might be crying (1973) and *A sort of peace* (1973), comprise a genuine and largely successful attempt to depict Glasgow before, during and just after World War II. The books are exhaustively researched and the characters, as the trilogy proceeds, strong and well-rounded. Catriona, the central character, matures over the three books to become an independent and credible woman, while, in *The breadmakers* itself, Sarah Fowler, driven to fatal retaliation by her unbearable mother-in-law, is handled with understanding and power.

But this was only the beginning for an author who, as the bibliography reveals, has since published nearly a score of novels – often in trilogies – set in various periods of Glasgow history, from the eighteenth century of the tobacco lords to the ever-popular depression years, and has set a trend followed by numerous other writers. Her novels do sometimes deal with contemporary Glasgow, and of these we may note *A very civilised man* (1982), with a restless, bored wife drifting into an affair with a charming and selfish university lecturer, as a good attempt at depicting the seldom-utilised middle-class face of the city.

Like George Friel, William McIlvanney had begun to publish before 1970, with two serious and powerful novels set mainly in Glasgow, *Remedy is none* (1966) and *A gift from Nessus* (1968). For some of his work he moves outside Glasgow (though there are connections and shared characters in many of his novels), but the Glasgow scene reappeared to great effect in the unexpected form of *Laidlaw* (1977). This gripping and literate police thriller – as it is on one level, though it is much more – fuses an absolutely authentic Glasgow background with a universal hero, the tough, vulnerable, unsettled and unsettling Detective-Inspector Laidlaw, who lives in the mind long after the book has been read. *Laidlaw* explores the Glasgow underworld as Laidlaw sees it, which is to say with considerable understanding and respect, and the character himself is further explored in *The papers of Tony Veitch* (1983) and *Strange loyalties* (1991), a sequence which, while a landmark in Glasgow crime fiction, is also a high point in Glasgow fiction as a whole.

If the 'seventies were significant years in Glasgow writing, the 'eighties and 'nineties have been remarkable. Judgments on the writers of these decades can only be provisional at present, since their work is still in progress. In completing the survey of Glasgow fiction for the second edition of this bibliography, we solemnly declared that 'at the moment of writing... the Glasgow novel is in full flower', but we could hardly have been more wrong. A glance at the chronological index will show how many blooms were still to come.

We spoke then of a 'remarkable quantitative increase in novels published', and this has continued, with ten, twelve or fifteen Glasgow novels in a year not uncommon. It would be disingenuous to claim that all these novels are great works of literature. Though (as before) we have not sorted the sheep from the goats, it can be seen that some of the quantitative increase is down to the fashion (as remarked in connection with the work of Margaret Thomson Davis) for producing family sagas in trilogies or quartets, and more can be attributed to the recent popularity of self-publishing, bringing to the shelves novels which a commercial publisher might not consider viable. These developments are perhaps a result, not a cause, of the flowering of Glasgow fiction.

But it has certainly flowered. We spoke in 1985 of the high quality of then-recent Glasgow novels, and of 'the fact that remarkably few fall into our well-worn categories of slum, gangland, urban kailyard, or (as it were) all-purpose proletarian novel. They are difficult to categorise at all: they have individuality and style.' In this, at least, we were right, and these latest decades in Glasgow fiction have been marked by individuality and style galore.

First, in 1981, came *Lanark*. Alasdair Gray's first novel has become something of a cult book; we can safely say that there had never been a Glasgow novel like it. It is almost two books: a realistic study of a young man growing up in the Glasgow of recent years, and a haunting, massive piece of science fiction or fantasy in which another young man, or the same one, moves through a dreadful city only too recognisable as a possible future Glasgow. Either book on its own would have been a worthy, but not unique, addition to the canon of the Glasgow novel. Combined, almost interleaved, as they are, the result is something completely different. Gray's genius has been further demonstrated during the 'eighties and 'nineties in novels and short story collections of great originality, reaching its peak (so far) in *1982, Janine* (1984), a fresh take on 'the matter of Scotland' in homage to Hugh MacDiarmid's *A drunk man looks at the thistle*, and in *Poor things* (1992), a pastiche Victorian novel which, among other things, looks into the situation of women then and now.

Apart from its own virtues, however, *Lanark* is immensely important in the story of Glasgow fiction. We cannot tell, of course, which of the 'eighties and 'nineties writers might have made a breakthrough in any case, but the appearance of *Lanark* seemed to empower and encourage Glasgow novelists; to demonstrate that a Glasgow novel could be offbeat and experimental, that the well-worn categories were things of the past. Within a few years Glasgow fiction had attracted the attention of the wider world.

The key figure, apart from Gray himself, was James Kelman, whose short stories had been published and anthologised throughout the 'seventies, but whose first substantial collection in Britain was *Not not while the giro* (1983). His first novel, *The busconductor Hines*, followed in 1984. Since then he has published both novels and short-story collections, each book exploring what has been recognised as 'Kelman's Glasgow': a downbeat, unsensationalised, grim Glasgow which is yet shot with humour and deep sensitivity. He is a master of the short story form, but those admirers who thought that his true forte were silenced by his brilliant fourth novel *How late it was, how late* (1994), which was awarded the Booker Prize.

The other novelists of the 'eighties and 'nineties are almost too numerous to list without resorting to catalogue format: section 10 of this bibliography gives a glimpse of their varied and often sparkling work. Frederic Lindsay began in 1984 with the complex, ambiguous political thriller *Brond*, following it with *Jill rips* (1987), a new slant on the Jack the Ripper story taking place in Maryhill. (Lindsay's later distinguished novels are not set in Glasgow.) Carl MacDougall, who like Kelman began with short stories, looks in his novel *The lights below* (1993) at the changes in his central character after a stretch in prison, but also in the Glasgow to which Andy returns. Frank Kuppner, primarily a poet, achieves something unique in his 'novel, of sorts' *A very quiet street* (1989), which interweaves reflections on the city, and some autobiography, with the story of a real-life murder mystery in Edwardian Glasgow.

Janice Galloway's first novel *The trick is to keep breathing* (1989) attracted immediate attention; while it is set in a bleak hinterland not specifically identifiable as Glasgow, her work, especially perhaps the short stories in *Blood* (1991), has an urban ambience and, at times, an unsettling surreal dimension. A. L. Kennedy's spare and probing short stories similarly bring a completely new voice to Glasgow fiction, but her masterpiece (so far – a caveat which has to recur in this section of our survey) is probably *So I am glad* (1995), in which a damaged young woman living in a Partick bedsitter is – psychologically – rescued and healed by a seventeenth-century Frenchman, none other than Cyrano de Bergerac.

Other books of the last few years demand to be mentioned. Chris Dolan's first collection of short stories, *Poor angels* (1995); Christopher Whyte's hilarious yet bitter *Euphemia McFarrigle and the laughing virgin* (1995); Bernard McLaverty's *Grace notes* (1997), in which Catherine, a young composer, works on a piece of music that offers at least a temporary resolution to the conflicts in her life; these are personal favourites to which a dozen more could be added. In previous editions of this bibliography we have sought 'the great Glasgow novel', but that phrase can probably be laid to rest now. We offer here the sketchiest of guides to the great Glasgow writing which has appeared and which, month by month, continues to appear.

The Glasgow Novel: a bibliography

I To 1699

1   BLACK, CHARLES STEWART. *Peter Meiklejohn: a tale of old Glasgow.* T. Werner Laurie,
      1925.

      A student at Glasgow College is sent down following a series of misadventures.
      The Glasgow atmosphere is slight and his subsequent romantic history has little
      Glasgow connection.

2   CHISNALL, EDWARD H. *The bell in the tree: thirty stories from Glasgow's past.*
      Collins and Radio Clyde, 1983.

      From scripts for a Radio Clyde series, these very short stories sketch the history of
      Glasgow from AD 543 to the 2080s. Followed by thirty more stories in *More stories
      from 'The bell in the tree'* (1984) and a further eighty in *Bell in the tree: the Glasgow
      story* (Edinburgh: Mainstream and Radio Clyde, 1990); no stories are duplicated.

3   GOVAN, ALLAN. *High adventure in Darien.* John Murray, 1936.

      Setting 1695-1700: the ill-fated Darien scheme as it affects certain Glasgow
      merchants and adventurers.

II 1700-1799

4   ALLAN, DOT. *Deepening river.* Jarrolds, 1932.

      The development of Clyde shipbuilding, told through the story of a family: sections
      1 and 2 are set in the eighteenth century, section 3 in 1913.

5   BLACK, WILLIAM. *James Merle: an autobiography.* Glasgow: Thomas Murray and
      Son, 1864.

      Set in upper Lanarkshire in the late eighteenth century, moving to Glasgow when
      Jamie, rebelling against his father's Calvinistic values, goes to the city in search of
      work. Lively descriptions of tobacco lords, gatherings in the Saracen's Head, and cows
      going home to their byres in the Cowcaddens.

6   DAVIS, MARGARET THOMSON. *The prince and the tobacco lords.* Allison and Busby,
      1976.

7   DAVIS, MARGARET THOMSON. *Roots of bondage.* Allison and Busby, 1977.

8   DAVIS, MARGARET THOMSON. *Scorpion in the fire.* Allison and Busby, 1977.

      Set in Glasgow and Virginia during and after the '45 rising; the intertwined stories
      of merchant's daughter Annabella and washerwoman's child Regina. Thoroughly
      researched; perhaps overpacked with local colour, though this is less obtrusive by
      the third volume of the trilogy.

9   DE HAVEN, AUDREY [pseud. of Dreda Boyd]. *The scarlet cloak.* Edinburgh:
      Blackwood, 1907.

      Set in Glasgow and Virginia, 1752-76, showing the growth of the tobacco trade
      and the changes it brings to Glasgow.

10   GALT, JOHN. *The entail: or, the lairds of Grippy.* Edinburgh: Blackwood, 1822.

A classic of Scottish literature and probably the first real 'Glasgow novel'; the obsession of an eighteenth-century Glasgow merchant with property and land.

11   HOGG, JAMES. *The private memoirs and confessions of a justified sinner.* Longman and Green, 1824.

This great novel is set mainly in Edinburgh, but an important encounter takes place in Glasgow: 'I hurried through the city, and sought again the private path through the field and wood of Finnieston ... Near one of the stiles, I perceived a young man sitting in a devout posture, reading a Bible.'

12   KYLE, ELISABETH [pseud. of Agnes M.R. Dunlop]. *The Tontine Belle.* Peter Davies, 1951.

Set partly in contemporary Glasgow, but with flashbacks to the eighteenth century.

13   [MILLS, GEORGE]. *Craigclutha: a Clydesdale story.* Glasgow: North British Railway and Shipping Journal, 1849.

Set mainly in Dumbarton area, but several chapters describe eighteenth-century Glasgow. First appeared as a serial in the above journal and published under the anagrammatic pseudonym there used, 'Mesrat Merligogels, Gent'.

14   SCOTT, WALTER. *Rob Roy.* Edinburgh: Constable, 1817.

Set around the 1715 Jacobite rising. See in particular the Glasgow merchant Bailie Nicol Jarvie, and the often-quoted description of Glasgow Cathedral.

15   SMOLLETT, TOBIAS. *The adventures of Roderick Random.* J. Osborn, 1748.

Semi-autobiographical picaresque novel, opening in Glasgow (where Smollett was educated and apprenticed), though the city is not identified by name.

16   SMOLLETT, TOBIAS. *The expedition of Humphry Clinker.* London: W. Johnston and Salisbury: B. Collins, 1771.

Picaresque epistolary novel including Glasgow in its itinerary.

17   STIRLING, JESSICA [pseud. of Hugh C. Rae]. *Lantern for the dark.* Hodder and Stoughton, 1992.

Setting 1787; a seventeen-year-old girl is in the Tolbooth charged with infanticide. The sequel *Shadows on the shore* (1993) is set mainly in Ayrshire.

18   STRAIN, EUPHANS H. *A prophet's reward.* Edinburgh: Blackwood, 1908.

Setting late eighteenth century, Glasgow and district.

III 1800-1836

19   DAVIS, MARGARET THOMSON. *The dark side of pleasure.* Allison and Busby, 1981.

Set around the end of William IV's reign and the beginning of Queen Victoria's. The story of fashionable Augusta who marries her father's coachman contrasts the comfortable life of Glasgow high society and the degradation in the nearby slums.

20   DUNCAN, HENRY. *The young south country weaver: or, A journey to Glasgow: a tale for the radicals.* 2nd ed. Edinburgh: Waugh and Innes, 1821.

The first edition was a privately printed tract. Set in 1819, when a young

Dumfriesshire weaver travels to Glasgow and lodges in Calton with his uncle, a noted radical. Long arguments attempt to convert him to the radical cause, but back in the more conservative countryside Uncle Daniel sees the error of his ways.

21   FREELAND, WILLIAM. *Love and treason.* Tinsley, 1871.
     Historical novel dealing with the Radical Rising in Glasgow, 1816-20.

22   GALT, JOHN. *The steamboat.* Edinburgh: Blackwood, 1822.
     Episodic novel narrated by a Glasgow merchant, set around 1820 (one adventure concerns the coronation of George IV). Originally stories in *Blackwood's Edinburgh Magazine.* Glasgow references also appear in *The gathering of the west* (1823).

23   HAMILTON, THOMAS. *The youth and manhood of Cyril Thornton.* Edinburgh: Blackwood, 1827.
     Includes scenes of early nineteenth-century Glasgow, particularly the university.

24   [LOCKHART, JOHN GIBSON] *Peter's letters to his kinsfolk, by Peter Morris the Odontist.* Edinburgh, 1819.
     Description of contemporary Scottish scene and customs in epistolary fiction form. Letters LXV-LXXII deal with Glasgow.

25   [MILLS, GEORGE] *The beggar's benison: or, A hero, without a name; but, with an aim. A Clydesdale story.* 2 v. Cassell, Petter and Galpin, 1866.
     Set in the early nineteenth century: a long and diverting Glasgow story following the hero's progress from slum child to businessman and Bailie.

26   MORRISON, NANCY BRYSSON. *When the wind blows.* Collins, 1937.
     Family story set in Glasgow 1825-36.

27   SCOTT, HONORIA [pseud. of Mrs Frazer]. *The vale of Clyde: a tale.* 2 v. J. Dick, 1810.
     Flora, brought up in a cottage in upper Clydesdale, goes to 'the capital of the Clyde' to visit her uncle, a well-off manufacturer with a mansion in George Square and 'a villa ... at the beautiful village of Port Dundas.' Interesting contemporary account of early nineteenth-century Glasgow society, including the *nouveau riche* Bailie and Mrs McDoit.

28   [TAYLOR, CHARLES] *The wildgoosechase: a narrative of real life, as exemplified in the history and travels of an ambulatory gentleman.* Glasgow: John Reid and Co.[etc], 1832.
     Mostly concerned with the hero's peregrinations in England, but there are interesting glimpses of contemporary Glasgow, which his landlady considers fully equal to London: 'Can we no ha'e every thing here we desire, if a body has only the bawbees?'

IV 1837-1900

29   [ALEXANDER, THOMAS, *jun.*]. *Charles Gordon, or, The mask of friendship: a tale of real life: by a student of the Glasgow University.* Glasgow: Dunn and Wright, 1865.
     A rather juvenile romance set in Glasgow about 1853. A contemporary review: 'To any of our readers who can stand a good deal of calf-love-making, we candidly

recommend *Charles Gordon*'.

30 ALLAN, DOT. *John Mathew, papermaker.* Hodder and Stoughton, [1948].
Setting 1860s. Probably based on the career of Allan's grandfather John Luke, papermaker in Denny; set mainly in that area, but moves to Glasgow for John Mathew's apprenticeship and later business meetings.

31 *Almost persuaded, or, Will love conquer?: a story of the Glasgow Plebiscite.* Glasgow: R. L. Holmes [etc.], 1887.
A temperance tale; originally published in serial form in support of the plebiscite, or referendum, held in March 1887 to ascertain Glasgow public opinion on the liquor trade. Love does conquer; Margaret refuses William's proposal because he is employed in his father's whisky warehouse, and he moves to his uncle's shipping firm in order to win her hand.

32 *Archie McNab, edited by he himself.* Glasgow: Holmes, 1888.
Collection of sketches originally published in the periodical *Quiz*.

33 [ARNOLD, FREDERICK]. *Alfred Leslie: a story of Glasgow life.* Glasgow: Thomas Murray and Son, 1856.
Showing Alfred the ropes at Glasgow University, the narrator touches fairly lightly on contemporary Glasgow scenes, society and customs. 'I have a very high opinion of the poorer classes of Glasgow... I walked down Bridgeton the other day behind two ragged mechanics who were discussing indices and surds'.

34 BERMANT, CHAIM. *The patriarch.* Weidenfeld, 1981.
Long, detailed Jewish family saga, opening in 1892 when Nahum Rabinowitz sails to Glasgow and changes his name to Raeburn. He founds a family and enters business: the fortunes of both enterprises are followed to 1968.

35 BLACK, WILLIAM. *White heather.* 3 v. Macmillan, 1885.
Essentially a Highland story, but the main characters, Ronald and his sister Maggie, move to live in Glasgow. Black's popular romantic novels typically have Highland or Hebridean settings, but Glasgow scenes tend to occur; see *A daughter of Heth* (1871) and *White wings* (1880).

36 BLAIR, EMMA [pseud. of Iain Blair]. *A most determined woman.* Michael Joseph, 1988.
A fairly typical 'Emma Blair' novel (see annotation at 143) except that the action begins at the earlier than usual date of 1890.

37 CLELAND, MARY [pseud. of Margot Wells]. *The two windows.* Hodder and Stoughton, 1922.

38 CLELAND, MARY [pseud. of Margot Wells]. *The sure traveller.* Hodder and Stoughton, [1923].
Parallel novels, covering the same period of time with many characters in common. In *The two windows* the waif Molly is befriended by a clever middle-class girl, Catherine, while *The sure traveller* is told from Catherine's point of view. Though both novels tend to the romantic, a sense of social concern removes them from the

kailyard class.

39 CULLEN, WILLIAM. *Uncle Archie: his nights with a nephew*. Glasgow: Gowans and Gray, 1925.

Reminiscences of a globe-trotting uncle, set about 1880-5. N.b. chapters XVI: 'University Reminiscences of the early '80s (Glasgow)', and XVII: 'Gladstone's Rectorial Address (1879)'.

40 DAVIDSON, JOHN. *The north wall*. Glasgow: Wilson and McCormick, 1885.

When unsuccessful novelist Maxwell Lee determines to 'create a novel', his brother-in-law goes out into the Glasgow streets and kidnaps a millionaire, thus 'causing a novel to happen' – this novel. More post-modern effects in the epilogue as Mr Lee provides a detailed description of his romantic leads Franklynne and Murielle, while roundly abusing the 'unimaginative readers' who require such assistance. (Reprinted, as *A practical novelist*, in *The great men and A practical novelist*, London, 1891.)

41 DAWSON, GEORGE HARDY. *The race for wealth: a Glasgow story*. Moffat: Robert Knight, 1891.

Novella-length account of a Glasgow merchant's striving to reach the heights of a villa in Pollokshields and its accompanying marks of gentility.

42 FERGUS, J.W. *Bill Broon, Territorial*. Kirkintilloch: D. Macleod, n.d.

Humorous urban kailyard sketches, reprinted from the periodical *The Bailie*.

43 FLEMING, ZACHARY, *Writer* [pseud. of Henry Johnston]. *Martha Spreull: being chapters in the life of a single wumman*. Glasgow: Wilson and McCormick, 1884.

Humorous dialect sketches, reprinted from the periodical *Quiz*, ostensibly as written by Martha Spreull. Of interest as a view of Glasgow about 1870.

44 FORD, ELBUR [pseud. of Eleanor Burford Hibbert]. *Flesh and the devil*. Werner Laurie, 1950.

Reconstruction of the Victorian Dr Pritchard murders, based on Roughead's *Notable Scottish Trials* volume. 'I hope my interpretation of his character will offer an explanation of what has hitherto been known as "murder without apparent motive".'

45 GORDON, C. J. *Jet Ford: a tale of our city*. Glasgow: John S. Marr, 1880.

A typical Victorian tract, in which a slum child rises via Sunday School to domestic service, a suitable marriage, and departure for the mission field. Displays, like *City echoes* (62), the philanthropic zeal which sought to alleviate the slum-dwellers' misery without considering its basic causes.

46 GRAY, ALASDAIR. *Poor things*. Bloomsbury, 1992.

Part pastiche of a Victorian novel, part a reworking of the Frankenstein story, part an essay in the unreliability of narrative, and more: a complex, rich novel set (mostly) in Victorian Glasgow, possibly Gray's masterpiece so far.

47 GUNN, NEIL M. *The serpent*. Faber and Faber, 1943.

Set mainly in the Highlands, but the early scenes in Victorian Glasgow are vital in the awakening of the young man's mind and body and his introduction to socialism and atheism, which he takes back to his native village.

48   HILL, PAMELA. *The incumbent.* Hodder and Stoughton, 1974.

The dark side of Victorian respectability: the two marriages and guilty secret of a stern and upright clergyman, in an unnamed city identifiable as Glasgow.

49   HOUSE, JACK. *House on the hill.* Glasgow: Richard Drew, 1981.

Based on a TV series depicting life in a Glasgow house, in six episodes set between 1878 and 1980.

50   *How Glasgow ceased to flourish: a tale of 1890.* Glasgow: Wilson and McCormick, 1884.

As the dates indicate, an early essay in science fiction.

51   HOWELLS, HARVEY. *Bide me fair.* New York: Simon and Schuster, 1968.

Family saga set in Glasgow (apart from holiday episodes on the island of Arran) tracing the fortunes of Robert and Harriet Boyd and their children from 1882 till after World War II.

52   KYLE, ELISABETH [pseud. of Agnes M. R. Dunlop]. *Douce.* Peter Davies, 1950.

A retelling of the Mary Queen of Scots story in the setting of Victorian Glasgow.

53   KYLE, ELISABETH [pseud. of Agnes M. R. Dunlop]. *Down the water.* Peter Davies, 1975.

Romantic novel set in 1900, dealing with the contemporary Glasgow School of artists.

54   LEVENAX, DAVID [pseud. of C. E. Beckett]. *Plain tales of the city and suburbs.* Glasgow: Jas. Hedderwick and Sons, n.d.

Humorous sketches: from internal evidence, may be asssigned to the late Victorian period.

55   LEWIS, MORAG. *Shusie: a Glesca love affair.* Glasgow: David Bryce, n.d.

A fine flower of the urban kailyard, in which a country lad working in Glasgow befriends an orphan gipsy girl and persuades two bachelor brothers and their Highland housekeeper to bring her up. When the gipsy is found to be an earl's daughter, further romance and adventure naturally follow.

56   *The life of an expert Glasgow pickpocket.* 3 parts. Glasgow: W. Scott, 1868.

The adventures of 'Tarry-fingered Jack', brought up around the Saltmarket and operating largely in Glasgow, though with some diversions in the wider arena of London.

57   McCRONE, GUY. *Wax fruit: the story of the Moorhouse family.* Constable, 1947.

58   McCRONE, GUY. *Aunt Bel.* Constable, 1949.

59   McCRONE, GUY. *The Hayburn family.* Constable, 1952.

Evocation of middle-class family life and background as the warm-hearted and innocently snobbish Bel Moorhouse propels her husband and family up the social ladder. *Wax fruit* is in three parts, of which part 1, 'Antimacassar city', was originally published in 1940; parts 2 and 3, 'The philistines' and 'The puritans', were not published separately before 1947, though they later appeared as individual paperbacks. *Wax fruit* is set in the period 1870-81, *Aunt Bel* in 1892 as Bel sets about arranging good marriages for her children, and *The Hayburn family* in 1900-1, moving to a younger generation of Moorhouse relations.

60   [MACMILLAN, ARCHIBALD]. *Jeems Kaye: his adventures and opinions.* Glasgow: W. and R. Holmes, [1903].

Collected edition of the humorous sketches reprinted from *The Bailie.* Previously appeared in book form as *Jeems Kaye, first series* (1883), *second series* (1886) and *third series* (1888).

61   MACRAE, DAVID. *George Harrington.* Glasgow: Scottish Temperance League, 1890.

Another temperance tract: Glasgow area in the 1860s.

62   NAISMITH, WILLIAM. *City echoes: or, Bitter cries from Glasgow.* Paisley: Alex. Gardner, 1884.

Another example of the Victorian tract: the story of two slum boys, the 'good' one who dies and the 'bad' one who survives to become a social reformer.

63   NIVEN, FREDERICK. *Justice of the peace.* Eveleigh Nash, 1914.

An early description of commercial Glasgow, bringing together the business world and the rising Glasgow school of art in the period 1890-1910. The relationship between the warehouseman and his artist son is drawn with great sympathy and understanding, and scene and atmosphere are sensitively observed and conveyed.

64   NIVEN, FREDERICK. *A tale that is told.* Collins, 1920.

A leisurely, gentle book tracing the life of a family over the period 1887-1913.

65   NIVEN, FREDERICK. *Mrs Barry.* Collins, 1933.

A widowed landlady's struggles with illness and hardship on behalf of her small son: undramatic, sometimes moving. The child's-eye view of their 'shipbuilding parish' is perceptive and true.

66   NIVEN, FREDERICK. *The staff at Simson's.* Collins, 1937.

Full treatment of the warehouse life sketched in his *Justice of the peace* (63); this 'documentary novel' covers the same period. The characters are neatly drawn if not deeply explored, and the picture of business Glasgow – not yet a common background in fiction – is impressively clear.

67   [PAE, DAVID] *The factory girl, or, The dark places of Glasgow. Showing evil over-ruled for good, iniquity punished, and virtue rewarded.* Aberdeen: William Lindsay and Lewis Smith, 1868.

A long and eventful tale of crime, body-snatching, religion and romance, perhaps summed up in its title. It had appeared as a serial in *People's Journal,* 1863-64, and an earlier version in book form had been published as *Lucy, the factory girl; or, The secrets of the Tontine Close* (Edinburgh, 1860).

68   PETRIE, GLEN. *Marianne.* Macmillan, 1977.

A Victorian murder mystery set in Cumbria, but largely inspired by the author's interest in the Glasgow murder trial, and particularly the apparent character, of Madeleine Smith. See also 78, 84 and 227.

69 QUIGLEY, JOHN. *King's royal*. Hamish Hamilton, 1975.

70 QUIGLEY, JOHN. *Queen's royal*. Hamish Hamilton, 1977.
Two long, solid books firmly set in the Victorian Glasgow of the whisky barons, contrasted with the distilleries from which their prosperity flows. The King family and their innovation of blended whisky form the catalyst for a story moving between business and romance. The third volume of the planned trilogy has not been published.

71 ROY, GEORGE. *Generalship*. Glasgow: James P. Forrester, 1858.
Told in the persona of a Glasgow wife discoursing on the 'generalship' needed to manage a husband. At first glance a forerunner of the 'urban kailyard' school, but probably written with satirical intention.

72 ROY, GEORGE. *Lectures and stories*. Glasgow: James P. Forrester, [1863].
Each of the six lectures on a worthy and improving theme is accompanied by an illustrative short story.

73 SLIMAN, DAVID. *Man-hunting: or, The hounds of the law*. Glasgow: Maclaren, [1888].
Author is 'an ex-detective', but these stories are fictionalised, even if based on fact.

74 STIRLING, JESSICA [pseud. of Hugh C. Rae]. *The good provider*. Hodder and Stoughton, 1988.

75 STIRLING, JESSICA [pseud. of Hugh C. Rae]. *The asking price*. Hodder and Stoughton, 1989.

76 STIRLING, JESSICA [pseud. of Hugh C. Rae]. *The wise child*. Hodder and Stoughton, 1990.

77 STIRLING, JESSICA [pseud. of Hugh C. Rae]. *The welcome light*. Hodder and Stoughton, 1990.
A quartet of novels covering some five years: Kirsty and Craig Nicholson leave Ayrshire for common-law marriage in late-Victorian Glasgow.

78 TAYLOR, ELIZABETH. *Blindpits*. 3 vols. Edinburgh: Edmonston and Douglas, 1868.
An accomplished novel of manners ('In this lofty habitation Mrs Barclay lived, and moaned, and bestowed her confidence on her neighbours ...') set in 'Ironburgh', probably Glasgow, and 'Heatherburgh', which may be Helensburgh. A family saga, but includes a murder mystery involving arsenic poisoning, which could have been inspired by the Madeleine Smith case a decade earlier; see also 68, 84 and 227.

79 TEADDY, *pseud. Sir Colin Cut-up & Co., or, As it is now-a-days*. Ward and Lock, 1857.
A curiosity in that its stated purpose is to demonstrate the hardship caused to the small independent milliner by the opening of 'millinery saloons' in department stores; amply illustrated by its heroine, who uncomplainingly works herself to death for her family.

80 *Typical cards*. Glasgow: A.W. Stenhouse, 1878.
Short, jocular sketches of 'types' of contemporary young men, their Glasgow connection to be deduced from occasional hints.

81 TYTLER, SARAH [pseud. of Henrietta Keddie]. *St Mungo's city*. Chatto and Windus, 1884.

The story of a self-made businessman and his family: a long novel conveying well the bustle of Victorian Glasgow. Notable for its drily humorous observation of society and accurate rendering of various styles of speech, including a rich and natural Scots.

82 WATSON, ROBERT. *Me – and Peter.* Sampson Low, [1926].

Adventures of two small boys, taking place largely in Pollokshaws while it was still an independent burgh (i.e. before 1912). From this and the tone of middle-aged reminiscence, the date of events may be set in the Victorian period.

83 WEBSTER, JAN. *Saturday city.* Collins, 1978.

The eventful years 1880-1918 in Glasgow are well conveyed in this middle book of a three-volume family saga. The first book, *Collier's row* (1977), and the third, *Beggarman's country* (1979), have some Glasgow scenes, but are mainly set in a Lanarkshire mining town.

84 WEST, PAMELA ELIZABETH. *Madeleine.* Severn House, 1984.

First published in USA 1983. A fictional version of the Madeleine Smith murder case; see also 68, 78 and 227.

85 WEYMAN, ALFRED J. *The dangerous man: a romance of present-day London and Glasgow life.* Roper and Drowley, 1888.

A Victorian novel of business and political intrigue: the rise and fall of an ambitious man.

86 WODEN, GEORGE [pseud. of G. S. Slaney]. *Mungo.* Hutchinson, [1932].

A family story covering the period c. 1890-1930: the best evocation of Glasgow is in the earlier chapters, when young John Mungo is starting in the textile trade. A notably human and balanced view of the rise of a Glasgow businessman. Woden's other novels are lighter in tone; see annotation at 208-209.

V 1901-1913

87 ALLAN, DOT. *The syrens.* Heinemann, 1921.

The rise to wealth of a Glasgow merchant, and his persistent longing for travel and adventure.

88 ALLAN, DOT. *Charity begins at home.* Robert Hale, 1958.

A lighter novel than her earlier work, covering a period from the Edwardian era to the mid-twenties.

89 BELL, J. J. *Wee Macgreegor.* Glasgow: The Scots Pictorial Publishing Co., [1902].

90 BELL, J. J. *Wee Macgreegor again: a sequel.* Glasgow: The Scots Pictorial Publishing Co., [1904].

Light, humorous and pleasantly sentimental sketches of a small boy in a Glasgow working-class family. Enormously popular from their original appearance in the Glasgow *Evening Times*, 1901-2. Several further sequels (see 94 and 125). In addition Bell attempted to repeat the successful formula in many other books, some set in Glasgow: e.g. *The nickums* (Glasgow: Gowans and Gray, 1923). These lack, however, the freshness of *Wee Macgreegor.* A connected curiosity is *Mair Macjigger* by Joseph W. Simpson (Glasgow: Gowans and Gray, 1903), a not unskilful parody of *Wee Macgreegor*, hitting also at other contemporary literary names including Sherlock Holmes and Neil Munro.

91   BELL, J. J. *Ethel.* Edinburgh: John Menzies, 1903.
    Heavily facetious conversations between a diffident young man and his dashing girl-friend.

92   BELL, J. J. *Thou fool.* Hodder and Stoughton, 1907.
    Partly set in Glasgow, this is a rather more serious novel than Bell's usual work.

93   BELL, J. J. *Whither thou goest.* Hodder and Stoughton, 1908.
    Largely set in 'Fairport' (Bell's fictional Helensburgh), where the orphaned heiress Ruth Lennox lives, but her matchmaking aunt is a Kelvinside matron of the period in full array.

94   BELL, J. J. *Courtin' Christina.* Hodder and Stoughton, 1913.
    A double sequel, to *Wee Macgreegor* (89, 90) and *Oh! Christina!* (1909), which is not set in Glasgow. The love story of Macgreegor, now an apprentice house-painter, and his female counterpart, the *enfant terrible* Christina.

95   BLAIR, JOHN, *pseud. Jean.* Maclaren, 1906.
    The story of a factory girl: a very early and impressive essay in realism, its unpatronising view of working-class life most unusual in its period. In 1907 a second work by John Blair, *Jake,* 'a volume of East End sketches', was announced as shortly to be published by Sands, but no copy of this book, nor evidence of its actual publication, has been found.

96   CAMPBELL, ROBERT W. *Jimmy McCallum.* Edinburgh: Chambers, 1921.
    Account of a little boy and his friends in pre-1914 Glasgow; their enrolment and adventures with the Boys' Brigade, and eventual enlistment and heroism in World War I as the B. B. Battalion. Told in Campbell's uniquely patronising tone; see also his 'Spud Tamson' books (128, 129, 153).

97   CARSWELL, CATHERINE. *Open the door!* Andrew Melrose, 1920.
    A strong novel of a woman's life and emotions, particularly honest for its time, and little dated. The title may refer to Joanna's discovery of sexual freedom, or to her escape from her Calvinistic middle-class background, which, with the West End scene and atmosphere, is well conveyed.

98   CARSWELL, CATHERINE. *The camomile: an invention.* Chatto and Windus, 1922.
    Characters from *Open the door!* (97) appear in minor roles in this epistolary novel. The heroine rebels similarly, if less drastically, against the middle-class philistinism of her home; a strong comment on the contemporary position of the woman writer.

99   CRONIN, A. J. *Three loves.* Gollancz, 1932.
    A somewhat pedestrian story of a woman's life; partly set in Glasgow. Of Cronin's many other novels, *A song of sixpence* (1964) has a Glasgow background but little depth: his 'Levenford' (Dumbarton) novels, such as *Hatter's castle* (1931), *The green years* (1945), and *Shannon's way* (1948), also havee Glasgow connections.

100 DOUGLAS, O. [pseud. of Anna Buchan]. *The Setons*. Hodder and Stoughton, 1917.

A pleasant story of a minister's daughter keeping house for her widowed father, and her gentle romance. Most of the action takes place in 1913, but the effects of World War I are not avoided in the closing chapters. Sharp but sympathetic observation of the *petit bourgeois* parishioners. The same author's *Ann and her mother* (1922), a largely autobiographical novel, touches on manse life at a slightly earlier period.

101 ECCOTT, W. J. *The second city*. Edinburgh: Blackwood, 1912.

An implausible urban kailyard novel, its plot involving the revelation of a poor but honest young lawyer as the illegitimate son of a highly respected sheriff. Has a certain value as a picture of wholly conventional middle-class Edwardian society, and of the petty intrigues of municipal politics.

102 FALCONER, ERIC. *Droll Glasgow, or, The humours of life in St Mungo*. Glasgow: Frederick W. Wilson, 1905.

Ostensibly humorous sketches in the form of 'stairhead gossip', rather too uniformly malicious for modern taste.

103 FERGUS, BLYTHSWOOD [pseud. of William Fergus]. *The barmaid: and what became of her*. Glasgow: R. Kirkland, 1902.

Romantic tale of the love and misadventures of a girl from the north: set partly in Glasgow, where she works as a barmaid. Written, according to the preface, with the aim of restoring the good name of the barmaid as a class, by showing 'what excellencies are found amongst those who, at railway stations and in restaurants, minister to the physical wants of the multitude'.

104 FERGUS, BLYTHSWOOD [pseud. of William Fergus] *Satan on holiday*. Glasgow: William Hodge, [1903].

Fantasy: the devil (in person) afoot in Glasgow, including a visit to the 1901 Exhibition.

105 GAITENS, EDWARD. *Growing up, and other stories*. Jonathan Cape, 1942.

Ten short stories, set before and during World War I, six of which later became chapters in *Dance of the apprentices* (106). Beautifully written; combines realism with a feeling for something beyond the mean streets of Gorbals.

106 GAITENS, EDWARD. *Dance of the apprentices*. Glasgow: William Maclellan, 1948.

A novel dealing with the same characters as *Growing up* (105) but carrying their stories on to about 1930. The best chapters, however, are the earlier ones, taken with little adaptation from *Growing up*. The book is episodic and technically awkward, but has great warmth, realism and vitality.

107 KUPPNER, FRANK. *A very quiet street*. Edinburgh: Polygon, 1989.

Subtitled 'A novel, of sorts', this unique contribution to Glasgow literature interweaves the story of the Oscar Slater murder case from 1908 with Kuppner's contemporary reflections. See also *Something very like murder* (182). *Life on a dead planet* (1996) has an even more tenuous claim to be called a Glasgow novel, but should be read for the full picture (so far) of Kuppner's treatment of the city.

108 KYLE, ELISABETH [pseud. of Agnes M. R. Dunlop]. *Free as air.* Peter Davies, 1974.
  Light romantic mystery set in 1912, with good atmosphere of West End Glasgow.

109 LAVIN, JOHN J. *Compass of youth.* Museum Press, 1953.
  A boy growing up in the east end of Glasgow and going to work in the local tannery. A vivid, well-written book, evoking the sights and sounds of 'The Square' and telling the stories of the assorted neighbours: the dialogue at times reaches a remarkable pitch of strength and tension.

110 McCRONE, GUY. *James and Charlotte.* Constable, 1955.
  A light story, told in flashback form, beginning with a romance and elopement at the 1901 Glasgow Exhibition and continuing to the present.

111 McCULLOCH, DAVID. *The swinging tub.* Hodder and Stoughton, 1917.
  Comic and sentimental story of a Glasgow-Irish docker, with, however, touches of realism – references to strikes and working conditions – unusual at this date.

112 MacGILL, PATRICK. *Children of the dead end: the autobiography of a navvy.* Herbert Jenkins, 1914.

113 MacGILL, PATRICK. *The rat-pit.* Herbert Jenkins, 1915.
  Parallel novels. The first follows the itinerant navvy Dermod Flynn from Ireland to Scotland, finally to Glasgow, in search of his sweetheart Norah; the second covers the same period of time, and in some cases exactly the same scenes, from Norah's viewpoint. Grim scenes in the slums and in the female lodging-house known as 'the rat-pit'.

114 MUIR, EDWIN. *Poor Tom.* Dent, 1932.
  Mainly concerned with a young man's reactions and guilt feelings towards his brother's illness and death: notable for its sensitive observation of slum Glasgow. Muir says that the characters and main situation are purely fictional, but parallels can be seen between *Poor Tom* and the early chapters of his *Autobiography* (1954: expansion of *The story and the fable*, 1940).

115 MUNRO, NEIL [Hugh Foulis, pseud.]. *Erchie, my droll friend.* Edinburgh: Blackwood, 1904.
  Sketches embodying the reminiscences of a Glasgow waiter: tending to the urban kailyard style, but with genuine quiet humour and sharp observation of the contemporary scene. A new annotated edition, *Erchie and Jimmy Swan* (Edinburgh: Birlinn, 1993), includes 52 previously uncollected Erchie sketches in addition to the original 29.

116 MUNRO, NEIL [Hugh Foulis, pseud.]. *Jimmy Swan, the joy traveller.* Edinburgh: Blackwood, 1917.
  Sketches of the adventures of a commercial traveller, not all set in Glasgow but with several glimpses of city scenes. *Erchie and Jimmy Swan* (see annotation at 115) includes 7 previously uncollected Jimmy Swan sketches in addition to the original 30.

117 MURRAY, DAVID CHRISTIE. *In his grip.* John Long, [1907].

Respected and upright Glasgow businessman is tempted by financial losses to unethical dealings with a parcel of uncut diamonds entrusted to him by a dying friend.

118 NIVEN, FREDERICK. *The three Marys.* Collins, 1930.

The life of an artist: set only partly in Glasgow, but this part includes his brief but important encounter with 'the second Mary', a factory girl living in a grim slum.

119 RAMSAY, THOMAS. *The wee doctor: via connubialis vera.* Felling-on-Tyne: Walter Scott Publishing Company, 1908.

A curiosity: an extraordinarily unromantic account of a young Glasgow merchant's search for a suitable wife. With the lady who best appears to meet his criteria, he seriously discusses whether they are in fact fit to embark on matrimony, and both undergo medical examinations before the wedding is fixed.

120 REVERMORT, J. A. *Cuthbert Learmont: a novel.* Constable, 1910.

A divinity student at Glasgow University in the first years of the century.

121 RITSON, JOSEPH. *Hugh Morrigill: street-arab.* R. Bryant, 1905.

Working-class Glasgow.

122 ROBERTSON, WILLIAM. *Morris Hume, detective.* Glasgow: William Hodge, [1903].

Short stories told by the 'Dr Watson' of a Glasgow private detective. Most were originally published in *People's Friend.*

123 SWAN, ANNIE S. *Love, the master key.* Hodder and Stoughton, [1905].

Interestingly set in a large Glasgow store, treating both the rich family which owns it, and the shy country girl who comes to work there and (not untypically for Swan) wins the owner's heart. Of her many other novels, *The guinea stamp* (1892) and *The stepmother* (1915) also deal with Glasgow.

124 WODEN, GEORGE [pseud. of G. W. Slaney]. *Voyage through life.* Hutchinson, [1940].

Period 1908-39: partly in the Monklands, but considerable sections set in Glasgow.

VI 1914-1919

125 BELL, J. J. *Wee Macgreegor enlists.* Hodder and Stoughton, 1915.

Further sequel to 89, 90, 94; Wee Macgreegor (by now engaged to Christina) in the army and on leave.

126 BLAIR, EMMA [pseud. of Iain Blair]. *The blackbird's tale.* Michael Joseph, 1989.

Another typical 'Emma Blair' novel (see annotation at 143), beginning in 1914 and following three generations of women in the bookselling and publishing trades.

127 BUCHAN, JOHN. *Mr Standfast.* Hodder and Stoughton, 1919.

Only one chapter is set in Glasgow, but this includes a vivid impression of Clydeside politics at the time of John Maclean.

128 CAMPBELL, ROBERT W. *Private Spud Tamson.* Edinburgh: Blackwood, 1915.

129 CAMPBELL, ROBERT W. *Sergt. Spud Tamson, V.C.* Hutchinson, [1918].

The World War I exploits of the 'Glesca Mileeshy ... a noble force, recruited from the Weary Willies and Never-works of the famous town of Glasgow'. A strange mixture of comedy and heroics. Spud Tamson has been called a 'national figure for a time', but is described throughout in an ineffably patronising way. See also 153.

130 DAVIS, MARGARET THOMSON. *A woman of property*. Century, 1991.

Set during World War I. Christina engineers a suitable marriage and proceeds to develop her flair for business, meanwhile trying to discourage her husband's continuing attraction to gipsy Annalie, whose daughter she finally takes into her own family. Concluded in *A sense of belonging* (163).

131 GALBRAITH, RUSSELL. *George Square 1919*.
Edinburgh: Mainstream, 1988.

Prosaic fictionalisation of the events culminating in the riot of 'Black Friday', which brought troops and tanks on to the streets of Glasgow.

132 HAY, JOHN MacDOUGALL. *Barnacles*. Constable, 1916.

An uneasy blend of romanticism in Glasgow and realism in the slums of Paisley, by the writer of the great West Highland novel *Gillespie* (1914). The realism has power and feeling notable at such an early date, though the Glasgow of the earlier scenes is less convincing.

133 KYLE, ELISABETH [pseud. of Agnes M. R. Dunlop]. *The Stark inheritance*. Peter Davies, 1979.

Set immediately after World War I, purporting to point out differences in social mores between Glasgow and Edinburgh, though this is rather superficially carried out.

134 MITCHELL, JAMES LESLIE. *The thirteenth disciple: being portrait and saga of Malcom Maudslay in his adventure through the dark corridor*. Jarrolds, 1931.

Covers the period 1898-1930, but the Glasgow chapters are set in 1914-15, seen as a brief episode in a dirty, rainy city. Mitchell (the real name of Lewis Grassic Gibbon) was a reporter in Glasgow for a short time, and the novel appears to be in part autobiographical.

135 TROCCHI, ALEXANDER. *Thongs*. Paris: Olympia Press, 1956.

A pornographic novel, originally published under the pseudonym Frances Lengel; later published New York, 1994. Begins in 1916 in the Gorbals, where the unfortunate heroine is the daughter of a Razor King, before moving to even more exotic locations.

VII 1920-1939

136 ALLAN, DOT. *Makeshift*. Andrew Melrose, [1928].

Realistic but sensitive account of a girl's growing up and her determination that her life – unlike her mother's – will not be a 'makeshift' affair; a clear feminist message, unusual in Glasgow fiction at this date.

137 ALLAN, DOT. *The Deans*. Jarrolds, [1929].

Family story: the father an unsuccessful house-painter, the son and daughter with ambitions to rise in the world. There is evidence of an attempt at something more realistic than a simple romance, for instance in the character of the mother, who tries to earn money for her family by illegal means.

138 ALLAN, DOT. *Hunger march.* Hutchinson, [1934].

Covers one day in the depression years, which sees a hunger march of the Glasgow unemployed: a novel of social concern, slightly predating and comparable to the better-known 'depression' novels of Barke (140) and Blake (147).

139 BARKE, JAMES. *The world his pillow.* Collins, 1933.

Set largely in the Highlands, but the sections 'Bundle and go' and 'Disinherited' treat of a countryman's impressions of Glasgow, a theme to which Barke returned later in *The land of the leal* (141).

140 BARKE, JAMES. *Major operation.* Collins, 1936.

An important 'proletarian' novel, presenting two opposite points of view by the device of bringing together a Glasgow businessman and a shipyard workers' leader in the same hospital ward. The argument tends to outweigh the story, but there are fine angry descriptive passages on the slums and a city heatwave.

141 BARKE, JAMES. *The land of the leal.* Collins, 1939.

A family's story covering 1820-1938, as they move from Galloway to the Borders, Fife, and finally Glasgow, where the section 'Within the city walls', 1919-38, stresses the impact of city life, depression and unemployment on country people. The novel is based on the story of Barke's own family; see his autobiographical *The green hills far away* (1940).

142 BELL, J. J. *The braw bailie.* Ward, Lock, 1925.

Urban kailyard stories, surviving tenaciously in the era of the realistic novel.

143 BLAIR, EMMA [pseud. of Iain Blair]. *Where no man cries.* Arrow Books, 1982.

Most of the numerous 'Emma Blair' novels set in Glasgow may suitably be grouped together here. *Where no man cries*, covering 1921-47, packs in every known Glasgow fiction cliché: class conflict, sectarian violence, poor boy's rise to tycoon, and his humiliation of the works owner who cheated his widowed mother out of compensation. Later titles, though not sequels, follow a simple (and evidently successful) formula involving the depression years, a stereotyped Glasgow, a passionate heroine and a joyless eroticism. They include *Nellie Wildchild* (1983), *Hester Dark* (1984), *The princess of Poor Street* (1986), *When dreams come true* (1987), and *Maggie Jordan* (1990). See also 36 and 126, which begin in an earlier period but manage to touch on the depression as they go on.

144 BLAKE, GEORGE. *Mince Collop Close.* Grant Richards, 1923.

Blake's first novel, a melodramatic and episodic book featuring an implausible female gang-leader. Its strong point is its full and accurate description of Cowcaddens slums: Blake's journalistic gift was at this time better developed than his powers as a novelist.

145 BLAKE, GEORGE. *The wild men.* Grant Richards, 1925.

More realistic than *Mince Collop Close* (144). A story of Bolshevism, and of two revolutionaries, father and son.

146 BLAKE, GEORGE. *Young Malcolm*. Constable, 1926.

The progress of a lad o' parts from school to university and research: deliberately unsensational, but at times verging uneasily on the sentimental.

147 BLAKE, GEORGE. *The shipbuilders*. Faber and Faber, 1935.

One of the key novels of the depression period: the closing of a shipyard, and its effect on Leslie Pagan, the owner's son, and Danny Shields, a riveter. A sympathetic and full picture (though Blake himself was later dissatisfied with the result) of the contrasting faces of Glasgow, not only thugs and poverty but the cosiness of tenement life and the comradeship of pubs and football matches.

148 BLAKE, GEORGE. *David and Joanna*. Faber and Faber, 1936.

An unemployed boy and his girl-friend spend an idyllic summer camping in the Highlands: winter brings them back to Glasgow, but not, it is implied, to conventional genteel-poor city life. Notable for its air of youthful idealism and the picture of mass escape, by means of cycling and hiking, from the depression-gripped city.

149 BLAKE, GEORGE. *The westering sun*. Collins, 1946.

While most of the book is set in 'Garvel' (Greenock), the last three chapters show a spinster daughter breaking free in 1918 from her conventional family, to live in Glasgow, set up a chain of restaurants, and become involved in the unemployment of the thirties and the blitzes of World War II. An earlier book about the same family, *The constant star* (1945), has a Greenock setting.

150 BUCHAN, JOHN. *Huntingtower*. Hodder and Stoughton, 1922.

Romantic adventure of a retired Glasgow shopkeeper and a band of street urchins, the Gorbals Diehards: a somewhat patronising and unrealistic view of slum children. The sequel, *Castle Gay* (1930), has only a tenuous connection with Glasgow.

151 CAMPBELL, ROBERT W. *Snooker Tam of the Cathcart Railway*. Edinburgh: Chambers, 1919.

Broadly humorous sketches about the Cathcart Circle, then as now the Glasgow commuters' railway line: another example of urban kailyard surviving World War I almost intact.

152 CAMPBELL, ROBERT W. *Winnie McLeod*. Hutchinson, [1920].

The story of a Glasgow typist: verging on the light romance, but an interestingly early appearance of the emancipated 'working girl'.

153 CAMPBELL, ROBERT W. *Spud Tamson out west*. Edinburgh: Chambers, [1924].

Set in Canada, where the plucky Spud has joined the Mounties, but strongly linked to Glasgow through the reminiscences of other exiles whom he meets. Similar in tone to earlier books about the character (see 128, 129) and continued in *Spud Tamson's pit* (1926), in which our hero returns to Scotland to aid the mining village of Auchagree in its time of trouble.

154 CARRUTHERS, JOHN [pseud. of J. Y. T. Greig]. *The virgin wife*. Jonathan Cape, 1925.

An uneven, wordy, but thoughtful novel: the hero and his frigid wife are a little stilted, but there is real vitality in his Glasgow girl-friend, Ethel, and the enigmatic Highlander MacLeod. Partly set in Glasgow, beginning and ending in Peter's lodgings in the university district: the same background appears briefly in the author's *A man beset* (1927).

155 COCKBURN, JOHN. *Tenement: a novel of Glasgow life.* Edinburgh: Blackwood, 1925.
An early example of the realistic treatment of slum life: accurate and thoughtful, but erring in the direction of monotony.

156 CONNINGTON, J. J. [pseud. of A. W. Stewart] *Nordenholt's million.* 1923.
When nitrogen-destroying bacteria devastate the world's vegetation, a Nitrogen Area, its headquarters in Glasgow University, is set up. A hand-picked population is to resolve the crisis and carry on the human race. An interesting item in the small corpus of Glasgow science fiction.

157 CRAIG, ROBERT. *Lucy Flockhart.* John Murray, 1931.
A girl comes to Glasgow to seek her fortune, still an unusual feminine role for its time: her love-story and discovery of spiritual freedom.

158 CRAIG, ROBERT. *O people!* John Murray, 1932.
A solitary man, obsessed with the vision of Scotland in the League of Nations, finds his ideas and eloquence diverted to the cause of a local by-election. An over-romantic, unevenly written book, but with some neatly observed Glasgow scenes and humour in the political passages.

159 CRAWFORD, ARCHIBALD. *Tartan shirts.* Putnam, 1936.
An insubstantial story about great financial schemes in the shirt-making business: laboriously humorous, with the air of a private joke.

160 CRONIN, A. J. *The minstrel boy.* Gollancz, 1975.
Partly set in Glasgow in the 1920s, but the hero's schooldays at the Jesuit-run 'St Ignatius' lack credibility, as does his later career as priest, husband, singer and missionary.

161 DAVIS, MARGARET THOMSON. *The breadmakers.* Allison and Busby, 1972.
Setting Govan tenement life in the 1930s, 'human interest' somewhat outweighing political and economic questions. The first novel in a trilogy; World War II and post-war austerity are spanned by the sequels, *A baby might be crying* (214) and *A sort of peace* (236).

162 DAVIS, MARGARET THOMSON. *Rag woman, rich woman.* Century Hutchinson, 1987.
Setting 1920s; rag woman's daughter Rory is betrayed by handsome intellectual Matthew, but recovers to build up a successful garment business. The first novel in a trilogy; continued in *Daughters and mothers* (237) and *Wounds of war* (238).

163 DAVIS, MARGARET THOMSON. *A sense of belonging.* Century, 1993.
Sequel to *A woman of property* (130), set in the 1930s and the opening years of World War II; concludes the story of Annalie and her daughter Elizabeth, now grown up and aware of her true parentage.

164 DOUGLAS, O. [pseud. of Anna Buchan]. *Eliza for common.* Hodder and Stoughton, 1928.

A gently romantic book set in a Glasgow manse just after World War I.

165 FRASER, CHRISTINE MARION. *King's close.* HarperCollins, 1991.

166 FRASER, CHRISTINE MARION. *King's farewell.* HarperCollins, 1993.

Fourth and fifth novels in a saga (the first three are not set in Glasgow) which follows Evie Grant and her family from rural Aberdeenshire to Govan in the 1920s and 1930s.

167 FRIEL, GEORGE. *A friend of humanity.* Edinburgh: Polygon, 1992.

A posthumous collection of Friel's fine short stories, written over several decades and set largely in the 1920s and 1930s.

168 GAVIN, CATHERINE. *Clyde valley.* Arthur Barker, 1938.

The love affair of a young woman novelist and an unhappily married man: the scandal ruins his political career and their elopement ends in tragedy. Moments of naiveté and over-writing, but strong passages on the emotions of the heroine and her jealous mother. Good on the sordid atmosphere of the hustings, with sectarianism and politics intermixed. A sequel, *The hostile shore* (1940), is not set in Glasgow.

169 GOODCHILD, GEORGE, *and* ROBERTS, C. E. BECHHOFER. *The dear old gentleman.* Jarrolds, 1936.

A reconstruction, set in the 1930s, of the nineteenth-century Jessie McLachlan murder case; follows the details closely, though names are changed, and goes on to postulate a confession and explanation of motive from the master of the house, in real life almost certainly culpable but legally unsmirched.

170 GUNN, NEIL M. *Wild geese overhead.* Faber and Faber, 1939.

A young newspaperman takes lodgings in the country outside Glasgow; the contrast throws into sharp relief his view of the slums and the newspaper world. Gunn, more usually regarded as a Highland writer, here depicts the city with a harsh poetic realism.

171 HAMILTON, MARGARET. *Bull's penny.* Macgibbon and Kee, 1950.

A true 'proletarian novel', concerned throughout with working people, which takes its protagonist from a late nineteenth-century childhood on Arran to the urban west of Scotland ('Fairniehead', possibly Barrhead, and Glasgow). The urban sequences span the 'twenties and 'thirties, with scenes in both World Wars. Both narrative and dialogue are in a fluent and natural Scots.

172 HANLEY, CLIFFORD. *Another street, another dance.* Edinburgh: Mainstream Publishing, 1983.

Hanley's major attempt to show Glasgow during the period 1926-45, centred on Hebridean Meg Macrae, who retains a calm integrity through two marriages, family crises, depression and war.

173 HASSETT, MARGARET [pseud. of Kathleen Daly]. *Educating Elizabeth.* Longmans, Green, 1937.

Humorous story of a young headmistress's troubles with her staff in a girls' school in a large Scottish city, plausibly Glasgow. Continued in *Beezer's end* (217).

174 HAYNES, DOROTHY K. *The Gibsons of Glasgow*. In Aistrop, Jack, ed., *Triad two*. Dennis Dobson, 1947.
> Naught for anyone's comfort in this novella following John Gibson and his family from 1915, when he returns crippled from World War I, to the middle of World War II, when he is reluctantly persuaded to go into a home. Accurate, observant and grim.

175 HENDERSON, WILLIAM. *King of the Gorbals*. New English Library, 1973.
> Documentary fiction about a boxer, 'Benny Morrison', whose life parallels that of the real Benny Lynch. Of negligible literary value, but tries in its way to capture a Glasgow legend.

176 HENDRY, J. F. *Fernie brae: a Scottish childhood*. Glasgow: William Maclellan, 1947.
> Sensitive, impressionistic child's-eye view of tenement life and school, continuing to adolescent problems and university.

177 HIGHLANDS, ALEXANDER. *The dark horizon*. Jarrolds, 1971.
> Covers the years 1937-41: the effects of depression and war on two Clydeside families. Plot and characterisation are less notable than the accurate detail of social conditions and the shipbuilding trade, vividly recalled and recorded by an author who had been blind since 1961.

178 HILL, PAMELA. *The sisters*. Robert Hale, 1986.
> The story of three Glasgow spinsters, spanning mid-1920s to early 1950s, told largely by a young girl who lives with them; a short novel with a quality of bleak truth.

179 HUNTER, STEWART. *This good company*. Nicholson and Watson, 1946.
> A boy rejects the family textile business to study art in Glasgow and on the Continent.

180 KANE, ALBERT. *The Glaswegian*. Braunton: Merlin, 1983.
> Fictionalised memoir considering class and sectarian conflict in 1920s Glasgow: middle-class Protestant university student Neil is bemused by the General Strike of 1926 and by his doomed love for Catholic fellow-student Maureen. *But the memory lingers on* (1987) calls itself a sequel, but is straight autobiography.

181 KEENAN, JIM. *Glasgow forever*. Haddington: Albyn Press, 1988.
> Begins as a memoir of childhood in 1930s Glasgow; proceeds, without much literary distinction, to a fictional City Revolution in the 1940s, when flags of anarchism and socialism are hoisted over the City Chambers.

182 KUPPNER, FRANK. *Something very like murder*. Edinburgh: Polygon, 1994.
> Deals with the Bertie Willox murder case of 1929 in a similar technique to that of *A very quiet street* (107).

183 LAMBERT, DAVID. *He must so live*. Lawrence and Wishart, 1956.

184 LAMBERT, DAVID. *No time for sleeping*. Lawrence and Wishart, 1958.
> Factory and national politics in a Clydeside foundry: reminiscent of the 'proletarian'

novels of the 'thirties, though published some twenty years later.

185 McARTHUR, ALEXANDER *and* LONG, H. KINGSLEY. *No mean city: a story of the Glasgow slums.* Longmans, Green, 1935.

The famous, or notorious, Gorbals novel, compiled with the help of Long (a journalist) from the mass of McArthur's reminiscences and writings. Presents a highly-coloured and probably over-simplified view of Gorbals life in the 'twenties, yet with a fair amount of demonstrably accurate social detail. No other novels were published during McArthur's lifetime. In addition to *No bad money* (186), *The blackmailer* (Glasgow: E. Rennie, 1948) was published after his death. The publishing history of *The blackmailer* is obscure and few copies appear to have survived.

186 McARTHUR, ALEXANDER *and* WATTS, PETER. *No bad money.* Transworld Publishers, 1969.

Compiled from fragmentary posthumous papers of McArthur's; hence largely written by the co-author, Watts. As in *No mean city* (185), social comment is rather obscured by sensationalism.

187 MacCOLLA, FIONN [pseud. of Thomas Douglas MacDonald]. *The Albannach.* John Heritage, 1932.

This great Highland novel, set in the early 1920s, has striking Glasgow passages: the hero's first impressions when he comes to attend university, and later a powerful sequence culminating in a sick and distorted view of the city.

188 McCRONE, GUY. *The striped umbrella.* Constable, 1937.

The story of a Glasgow family after the death of their authoritarian father: his widow in particular finds hitherto unsuspected richness in life under the 'striped umbrellas' of France.

189 McKECHNIE, SAMUEL. *Prisoners of circumstance.* Sampson Low, [1934].

Near-slum tenement life: covers the period 1908-33, but basically a story of a family in the depression years.

190 McNEILLIE, JOHN. *Glasgow keelie.* Putnam, 1940.

Summed up by its title: an unrelievedly grim slum-gangland novel in the fashion set by *No mean city* (185).

191 MUIR, THOMAS. *The sea road.* Jarrolds, 1959.

Covers the period 1895-1930: a boy's upbringing with harsh relations in Cowal, and his escape to marine engineering in Glasgow. Apparently accurate, if pedestrian in style.

192 MUNRO, HUGH. *The Clydesiders.* Macdonald, 1961.

The depression and early war years as they affect one family, the father an unemployed shipyard worker. The mother is a strong portrait and the son's schooldays, adolescence and romance are sensitively drawn. Episodic in structure and therefore rather light in effect, but honest, authentic, and unsensational.

193 MUNRO, HUGH. *The keelie.* Robert Hale, 1978.

The story of a working-class Glasgow boy struggling (from the 1930s to the present) with lack of education and opportunity, to gain eventual, though brief, success as a writer.

194 NIVEN, FREDERICK. *The rich wife.* Collins, 1932.

A Glasgow woman looks back over some twenty years (c. 1910-30) during which, as daughter of a prosperous shipbuilder, she was married for her money by a selfish, conceited writer. After the stresses of her marriage, occurring away from Glasgow, she finds comfort and spiritual renewal in returning, as on a pilgrimage, to the South Side flat which was her childhood home.

195 PAIGE, FRANCES. [pseud. of May W. Martin]. *The Glasgow girls.* Harper Collins, 1994.

The three Mackintosh sisters (no relation to Charles Rennie Mackintosh, though reference is made to the original 'Glasgow girls', his contemporaries) are students at Glasgow School of Art in the 1930s, beginning a long romantic saga which is continued in *The painted ladies* (277), *The butterfly girl* (278) and *Kindred spirits* (391).

196 PRYDE, HELEN W. *The first book of the McFlannels.* Nelson, 1947.

This and its sequels (221, 279-281) consist of radio sketches in book form, on the life and times of a family in a Glasgow tenement: the prime example of the survival of urban kailyard, immensely popular in their day with radio audiences in Scotland.

197 REID, JOHN MACNAIR. *Homeward journey.* Edinburgh: Porpoise Press, 1934.

The slum/middle-class contrasts of contemporary Glasgow life are essential in the story of a girl's determination to escape from one milieu to another. An unsuccessful love-affair nevertheless helps a young man toward self-discovery.

198 REID, JOHN MACNAIR. *Judy from Crown Street.* Ilfracombe: Arthur H. Stockwell, 1970.

A posthumously published novel, treating, like *Homeward journey* (197), the division between middle-class and near-slum. There is maturity in the conception and presentation of Judy, and the character of Grannie is particularly sharp and sympathetic.

199 RUSSELL, JAMES ANDERSON. *The scorner's chair.* Loanhead: Macdonald Publishers, 1973.

Period 1934-40. Set in Glasgow (called Glasburgh) and Rutherglen (Glenruther). A divinity student at Glasgow University pursues research in Germany, attains professorship but attracts controversy; by the end he seems set to find peace and satisfaction rather in marriage and a teaching career.

200 SHIELS, EDWARD. *Gael over Glasgow.* Sheed and Ward, 1937.

A young Clydebank-Irish engineer growing up in the depression: the effects of unemployment and strike action on his idealism and loyalties. The happy ending to his dream of settling in the Highlands comes too pat, but the book as a whole is sensitive and honest, with vivid shipyard scenes.

201 STIRLING, JESSICA [pseud. of Hugh C. Rae]. *The penny wedding.* Hodder and Stoughton, 1994.

202 STIRLING, JESSICA [pseud. of Hugh C. Rae]. *The marrying kind.* Hodder and Stoughton, 1995.

> Two novels set in the 1930s and following the fortunes of a shipyard worker's family who move from Partick to a new 'garden suburb'.

203 SWAN, ANNIE S. *The land I love.* Ivor Nicholson and Watson, 1936.

> Fourteen short stories intended to illustrate 'the component parts of Scottish life'. Three of the stories have Glasgow or Clydeside settings.

204 TAIT, W. CUMMING. *The wise thrush.* Cassell, 1937.

> A young man's experiences: some good description of Glasgow and authentic dialogue.

205 WODEN, GEORGE [pseud. of G. W. Slaney]. *Tannenbrae.* Hutchinson, 1935.

206 WODEN, GEORGE [pseud. of G. W. Slaney]. *The bailie's tale.* Hutchinson, 1937.

207 WODEN, GEORGE [pseud. of G. W. Slaney]. *The Cathkin mystery.* Hutchinson, 1937.

208 WODEN, GEORGE [pseud. of G. W. Slaney]. *Happiness has no story.* Hutchinson, [1938].

209 WODEN, GEORGE [pseud. of G. W. Slaney]. *Helen enchanted.* Hutchinson, 1940.

> Woden's novels of this period, with the exception of his major work *Mungo* (86) and *Othersmith* (210), may well be considered together, since they are of interest less for any individual inspiration than for their number and solid average worth. They are firmly set in Glasgow: the author states in more than one preface that the topography is accurate though the characters are fictitious. They are notable for their retention of a middle-class background in a period when the trend was strongly towards the working-class and slum novel, while they remain slightly more substantial than the average urban kailyard work.

210 WODEN, GEORGE [pseud. of G. W. Slaney]. *Othersmith.* Hutchinson, [1936].

> Set in Glasgow and just outside: a man's memories of twenty-five years. More ambitious and rather more accomplished than the bulk of Woden's work. Contains an unexpectedly full and enthusiastic description of the interior of Glasgow Cathedral.

VIII 1939-1945

211 BARCLAY, JAMES. *Paras over the Barras.* Glasgow: Lang Syne Publishers, 1995.

212 BARCLAY, JAMES. *The second wave.* Glasgow: Lang Syne Publishers, 1996.

> The legendary Glasgow qualities of neighbourliness and humour relentlessly displayed in the East End during World War II.

213 BURROWES, JOHN. *Jamesie's people.* Edinburgh: Mainstream Publishing, 1984.

> A Gorbals story, opening with the killing of 'hard man' Jamesie Nelson in 1927, but primarily following the stories of his daughter Star, evacuated to the country in World War II and finding it hard to adjust to Gorbals society afterwards, and his brother Sammy who by the late 1940s has attained wealth and respectability in Pollokshields. Heavy with local description, somewhat to the exclusion of literary

style, but begins a trilogy interesting for its social comment on postwar Glasgow; see the sequels *Incomers* (230) and *Mother Glasgow* (231).

214 DAVIS, MARGARET THOMSON. *A baby might be crying.* Allison and Busby, 1973. Sequel to *The breadmakers* (161), following Catriona and her family through World War II. Continued in *A sort of peace* (236).

215 'DOMINIE' [pseud. of Jacob Morrison]. *The great trek: a school evacuation story.* Glasgow: Craig Wilson, 1941.
Fairly light and semi-romantic, but its theme of the wartime evacuation of city children to the country was little handled until *Guests of war* (218).

216 GUNN, NEIL M. *The lost chart.* Faber, 1949.
Story of espionage, set largely in Glasgow.

217 HASSETT, MARGARET [pseud. of Kathleen Daly]. *Beezer's end.* Longmans, Green, 1949.
The difficult First Assistant of *Educating Elizabeth* (173) has her own problems when part of the school is evacuated to the Highlands at the beginning of World War II.

218 JENKINS, ROBIN. *Guests of war.* Macdonald, 1956.
The evacuation of a slum school from 'Gowburgh' (recognisably Glasgow) in autumn 1939. The reactions of both sides are rendered with perceptive humour. In the fine gallery of Gowburgh women, the heroine Bell McShelvie is a portrait of exceptional strength and sensitivity.

219 McGHEE, BILL. *Cut and run.* Hammond, Hammond, 1962.
A sensational book of the gangland school: of negligible literary value, its one good point the accurately rendered slang and dialect.

220 McGINN, MATT. *Fry the little fishes.* Calder and Boyars, 1975.
Grim, humorous, partly autobiographical story of a boy at a Catholic approved school during World War II. Scenes of seamy wartime Glasgow provide a background to his attempted escape, which ends when – a topical black joke – he runs head-first into a baffle wall.

221 PRYDE, HELEN W. *The McFlannels see it through.* Nelson, 1948.
Wartime adventures of the McFlannel family (see 196, 279-281).

222 SCOTT, DOUGLAS. *Die for the queen.* Secker and Warburg, 1981.
A wartime spy/counterspy thriller, with the Germans trying to destroy the *Queen Elizabeth*.

223 WODEN, GEORGE [pseud. of G. W. Slaney]. *Dusk for dreams.* Hutchinson, 1941.

224 WODEN, GEORGE [pseud. of G. W. Slaney]. *Messenger-at-arms.* Hutchinson, 1947. Set in contemporary Glasgow: see annotation to 205-209.

IX 1946-1969

225 BERMANT, CHAIM. *Jericho sleep alone.* Chapman and Hall, 1964.
An adolescent boy's last year at school and his experiences in a kibbutz, from which

he returns with relief to the warm predictability of his Glasgow Jewish community. A perceptive and often very funny picture of first – and second-generation Glaswegians, determined that their children shall improve in social status.

226 BLAIR, EMMA [pseud. of Iain Blair]. *Jessie Gray.* Arrow Books, 1986.
A typical 'Emma Blair' novel (see annotation at 143), except that it is set between 1947 and the early 1960s.

227 BLAKE, GEORGE. *The Peacock palace.* Collins, 1958.
Promisingly fresh setting – an old house in the university district let out in rooms, and its multi-racial student population – but Blake is not quite at home in this milieu, and the book is eventually a history of the Peacock family, owners of the house, whose story has parallels with those of Madeleine Smith (see also 68, 78, 84) and the City of Glasgow Bank collapse.

228 BURGESS, MOIRA. *The day before tomorrow.* Collins, 1971.
The strength of this first novel probably lies not in the slightly intrusive thriller plot which links the small group of protagonists, but in the description of a hot summer week in a half-demolished slum district of the city, evoking character and atmosphere with a certain economy of style and an accurate ear for Glasgow speech.

229 BURGESS, MOIRA *and* WHYTE, HAMISH *eds. Streets of stone: a anthology of Glasgow short stories.* Edinburgh: Salamander Press, 1985.
Stories by 22 authors, the majority written post-World War II, representing Glasgow short fiction from the 1930s to the mid 1980s. Criteria for selection: 'perhaps ... the truthful depiction of some aspect of Glasgow life, or (less tangibly) the expression of some essential trait of Glasgow character'.

230 BURROWES, JOHN. *Incomers.* Edinburgh: Mainstream, 1987.

231 BURROWES, JOHN. *Mother Glasgow.* Edinburgh: Mainstream, 1991.
Sequels to *Jamesie's people* (213), continuing the story of the Nelson family against a background of changing social conditions in Glasgow. *Incomers* deals with Asian immigration during the 1950s. *Mother Glasgow* records the movement of Glaswegians during the 1960s, both by resettlement from slums to housing schemes and by emigration overseas.

232 CALVIN, HENRY [pseud. of Clifford Hanley]. *The system.* Hutchinson, 1962.
Thriller, opening and closing in Glasgow, with episodes set around Loch Lomond.

233 CALVIN, HENRY [pseud. of Clifford Hanley] *A nice friendly town.* Hutchinson, 1967.
Thriller set in Glasgow with much local detail: a country boy becomes involved with the Glasgow underworld.

234 CARLTON, ALEXANDER. *University sunrise.* Ossian Press, 1969.
A polemical autobiographical novel attacking administration and conditions in Glasgow University: of negligible literary value.

235 CRAWFORD, IAN. *Scare the gentle citizen.* Hammond, Hammond, 1966.
Murder story reaching its climax in The Mitchell Library.

236 DAVIS, MARGARET THOMSON. *A sort of peace.* Allison and Busby, 1973.

Sequel to *The breadmakers* (161) and *A baby might be crying* (214), completing the 'Breadmakers' trilogy in the aftermath of World War II.

237 DAVIS, MARGARET THOMSON. *Daughters and mothers*. Century Hutchinson, 1988.

238 DAVIS, MARGARET THOMSON. *Wounds of war*. Century, 1989.

Sequels to *Rag woman, rich woman* (162). *Daughters and mothers*, set immediately after World War II in Glasgow and Russia, carries on the story of Rory, now profiting from the black market; her friend Victoria, married to Matthew, who is now a Labour MP; and their respective families. *Wounds of war*, set in the 1960s, extends the families' history to grandson Harry, but includes a wider cast of characters and their involvement in the contemporary problems of post-war trauma, Ban the Bomb activities and American civil rights struggles.

239 DAVIS, MARGARET THOMSON. *Hold me forever*. Century, 1994.

240 DAVIS, MARGARET THOMSON. *Kiss me no more*. Century, 1995.

Setting 1950s/1960s; the first two novels of a trilogy. Andrina marries quiet Robert to please her narrowly religious mother, but continues to indulge a mutual obsession with her more exotic first lover Bernard. Concluded in *A kind of immortality* (319).

241 FORRESTER, LARRY. *Diamond beach*. Harrap, 1973.

Set in Africa, but contains reminiscences of Glasgow childhood.

242 FRIEL, GEORGE. *The bank of time*. Hutchinson New Authors, 1959.

The story of the youngest of three brothers, from boyhood and family relationships to first love.

243 FRIEL, GEORGE. *The boy who wanted peace*. John Calder, 1964.

A gang of small boys, led by a slow, dimly idealistic adolescent, find the proceeds of a bank robbery hidden in the school cellar. Percy, the leader, bands them together for secrecy, but internal rivalry soon arises, his vague gropings after knowledge and power giving way to the sharp quickness of a younger boy. Acute and humorous on the boys, but also asking questions about the perceived value of the money.

244 FRIEL, GEORGE. *Grace and Miss Partridge*. Calder and Boyars, 1969.

At first sight a story of tenement life, centring on the old woman Wee Annie with her obsession for ten-year-old Grace, and observing sharply and humorously the other neighbours and the life of the back-courts; yet much more than that with its Joycean wordplay and oblique exploration of Wee Annie's past, and the ambiguous position of the narrator.

245 FRIEL, GEORGE. *Mr Alfred M.A.* Calder and Boyars, 1972.

Impressive portrayal of a seedy, alcoholic, middle-aged schoolmaster whose transfer from a bad school to a worse one sets him on a final descent to near-senility. A striking dialogue towards the end between Mr Alfred and the Devil shifts the book startlingly into a new dimension.

246 FRIEL, GEORGE. *An empty house*. Calder and Boyars, 1974.

A slightly disappointing novel which starts slowly as a family saga, begins to grip as Adam sets up house with two drop-outs, but fades towards the end. Moments of good atmospheric description of derelict Glasgow. Though the imprint date is 1974, the book did not actually appear until spring 1975, after Friel's death.

247 HANLEY, CLIFFORD. *The taste of too much.* Hutchinson, 1960.

Adolescent boy's school and family relationships and first love: lightly written but recording the boy's feelings perceptively and truly. Set in a council housing scheme, still an unusual background for Glasgow fiction.

248 HANLEY, CLIFFORD. *Nothing but the best.* Hutchinson, 1964.

Tom Fletcher, brought up in depression-hit Renfrewshire, is now a successful businessman in 'sixties Glasgow. Under the lightness and humour there is sympathy in the treatment of Tom as he confronts a takeover bid and family problems following his wife's death.

249 HANLEY, CLIFFORD. *The red haired bitch.* Hutchinson, 1969.

Interweaves the staging of a Mary Queen of Scots musical with a gangland story: two promising themes, treated however with a certain superficiality.

250 HEALY, THOMAS. *It might have been Jerusalem.* Edinburgh: Polygon, 1991.

A tersely-written, grim short novel set in the Glasgow slums in the late 1950s.

251 HEALY, THOMAS. *Rolling.* Edinburgh: Polygon, 1992.

The central character is already a hard man and a drinker when he leaves Glasgow in the early 1960s, on an odyssey which takes him through several European countries and years of alcoholism.

252 HIND, ARCHIE. *The dear green place.* Hutchinson, 1966.

Described by the publishers as an 'autobiographical documentary novel': Mat Craig's struggles to reconcile his writing with his working-class origins and his family's expectations for him. Though perhaps uneven as a novel, because of long stretches of unrelieved political and philosophical musing by Mat, it contains passages of real power (such as the description of work in a slaughterhouse), evocations of the warmth and affection of tenement life, and some descriptions of Glasgow which succeed in blending scene, history and atmosphere to a degree seldom achieved. Regarded as seminal in the development of Glasgow fiction.

253 HUNTER, STEWART. *The happiest hour.* Collins, 1953.

A straightforward contemporary novel: a girl strikes out on her own by opening a shop.

254 JENKINS, ROBIN. *The changeling.* Macdonald, 1958.

A bright slum child and petty thief is befriended by a teacher and taken on a family holiday. His mother and friends follow, and the boy's despair at the realisation of the two irreconcilable ways of life leads to tragedy. Grim picture of modern slums, and humorous but truthful descriptions of school. Jenkins treats a similar theme in *A love of innocence* (1963), set on a Hebridean island, where the chance of a new life for orphan boys sent to foster-parents is overshadowed by the tragedy of their childhood in a Glasgow slum.

255 JENKINS, ROBIN. *A very Scotch affair.* Gollancz, 1968.

A fine novel giving equal weight to the Glasgow background – the 'ghetto' of Bridgeton, considered to doom its inhabitants to social inferiority – and the people in the foreground: the deeply selfish Mungo, his fat, common, loving wife Bess, and their family. Impressive in its observation and rendering of character.

256 KENNAWAY, JAMES. *The bells of Shoreditch.* Longmans, 1963.

Though set in London and dealing with City machinations, this novel is permeated by the Glasgow socialist ethos which has shaped the conscience of its heroine Stella Vass, faced with betraying either her beliefs or her husband.

257 KENNAWAY, JAMES. *The cost of living like this.* Longmans, 1969.

Posthumously published: a most accomplished novel, with a powerful theme – the main character is dying of cancer – deep insight into human relationships, and impeccable technique. Only part of the book is set in Glasgow, but the evocation of the city in a few pages is vivid and sympathetic.

258 KNOX, BILL. *Deadline for a dream.* Long, 1957.

The first in a long series of police-procedural novels featuring Thane and Moss, Glasgow CID officers. [Other titles listed in Whyte.]

259 McCRONE, GUY. *An independent young man.* Constable, 1961.

A wealthy Glasgow family's reaction to the appearance of an impecunious distant relative: somewhat superficial in setting, character and plot.

260 McGILL, JOHN. *That Rubens guy: stories from a Glasgow tenement.* Edinburgh: Mainstream, 1990.

A story sequence set during the 1950s: the interlinked adventures, ribald, rich and tragic, of the sixteen families who live up the close at No. 30. Many of the characters reappear in the novel *Giraffes* (261).

261 McGILL, JOHN. *Giraffes: a Glasgow novel.* Edinburgh: Mainstream, 1993.

Sequel to *That Rubens guy* (260) in which one of the tenement's young men takes up with middle-class schoolteacher Janet. He feels the inhabitants of her world to be 'Giraffes. Wombats. Black mambas. They're like something fae another planet to me', while his tenement neighbours have a similar effect on her.

262 McILVANNEY, WILLIAM. *Remedy is none.* Eyre and Spottiswoode, 1966.

The profound effect on a sensitive young man of his father's death in apparent failure. Largely set outwith Glasgow, but the opening scenes in the University Union are sharp and authentic.

263 McILVANNEY, WILLIAM. *A gift from Nessus.* Eyre and Spottiswoode, 1968.

The pressures on a man from his unsatisfactory marriage, uncongenial job and inconclusive love affair: his unheroic and partly disastrous, yet honest, attempt to straighten things out. A serious novel with passages of considerable power: the Glasgow background is well observed, though not essential to the book.

264 MAIR, ALISTAIR. *The ripening time.* Heinemann, 1970.

Begins well and realistically as a picture of an incompatible youthful marriage. Credibility fails as the book proceeds and the climax is not so much strong as melodramatic.

265 MALLOCH, PETER [pseud. of William Murdoch Duncan]. *The big steal*. Long, 1966.
Cited as an example of the many thrillers by Duncan, who used a wide variety of pseudonyms. [Other titles listed in Whyte.]

266 MILLER, HUGH. *The dissector*. New English Library, 1976.
Iain Ross surmounts his problems as a medical student from a working-class background (in part I, set in the 1960s) to become a brilliant forensic pathologist, given to solving cases which baffle the police (in part II, set in 1975). Miller's follow-up on similar lines, *The silent witnesses* (1984), is not set in Glasgow.

267 MILLER, JIMMY [i.e. James Fullerton Miller]. *Tenements as tall as ships*. Glasgow: Govan Workspace Ltd, 1992.
Eighteen stories set mainly in Govan during the 1950s, most written at that period. A first, posthumous, collection of Miller's fine short stories.

268 MIRVISH, ROBERT. *Woman in a room*. Alvin Redman, 1959.
Promises well at first in observation of the barrenness of bedsitter life, but essentially an undistinguished novel of a woman's unhappy marriage and subsequent love affair.

269 MIRVISH, ROBERT. *Holy Loch*. New York: William Sloan Associates, 1964.
Deals with the installation of the American Polaris submarine base near Glasgow after World War II, a topic otherwise not much handled in Glasgow fiction. Touches also on the bedsitter life treated in his earlier *Woman in a room* (268).

270 MORRISON, NANCY BRYSSON. *The following wind*. Hogarth Press, 1954.
Straightforward family novel set in contemporary Glasgow.

271 MORRISON, NANCY BRYSSON. *Thea*. Robert Hale, 1963.
A woman, returning to Glasgow some years after the death of her sister Thea, discovers unsuspected depths in Thea's apparently dull life, and confronts her own selfishness.

272 MUIR, MARIE. *Leezie Lindsay*. Macmillan, 1955.
The story of an unsuccessful marriage: essentially a light novel, partly set in Glasgow newspaper offices.

273 MUNRO, HUGH. *Who told Clutha?* Macdonald, 1958.
First of a series featuring Glasgow private detective Clutha. [Other titles listed in Whyte.]

274 NICOLSON, ROBERT. *Mrs Ross*. Constable, 1961.

275 NICOLSON, ROBERT. *A flight of steps*. Constable, 1966.
Two short novels, often humorous but full of understanding and compassion, dealing with a lonely, slightly deranged old woman living in an imaginary past and an almost equally hallucinatory present while her area of Glasgow is being pulled down around her. *Mrs Ross* was published in paperback (Penguin 1966) under the title *The whisperers*, and filmed under that title, with the location moved to Manchester.

276 OWENS, AGNES. *A working mother*. Bloomsbury, 1994.

Betty drinks too much as she copes with her war-damaged husband, their friend Brendan who is a source of unenthusiastic sex, and her creepy boss who offers well-paid 'extra typing duties'. Whether her story is real or illusory – she is relating it in hospital to a fellow-patient and 'Everything gets so jumbled up it's hard to know the truth' – this is an unsparing look at a woman's life.

277 PAIGE, FRANCES [pseud. of May W. Martin]. *The painted ladies*. Harper Collins, 1995.

278 PAIGE, FRANCES [pseud. of May W. Martin]. *The butterfly girl*. Harper Collins, 1995.
Sequels to *The Glasgow girls* (195), continuing the story of the Mackintosh sisters. *The painted ladies* is set during the 1950s in Glasgow, Spain and New York; *The butterfly girl*, set in Glasgow in 1968, moves to a younger generation with its central character, Anna's daughter Vanessa. The series concludes with *Kindred spirits* (391).

279 PRYDE, HELEN W. *McFlannels united*. Nelson, 1949.

280 PRYDE, HELEN W. *McFlannel family affairs*. Nelson, 1951.

281 PRYDE, HELEN W. *Maisie McFlannel's romance*. Nelson, 1951.
Further instalments of the McFlannel saga (see 196, 221).

282 QUIGLEY, JOHN. *The bitter lollipop*. Hutchinson, 1964.
A cynical young journalist turns from his innocent girlfriend to an affair with an older married woman; his extreme bitterness about life is hardly adequately motivated and the other characters are not explored in depth. There is a general atmosphere of seedy gloom about the setting, an unnamed city identifiable as Glasgow.

283 QUIGLEY, JOHN. *The golden stream*. Collins, 1970.
Detailed but pedestrian novel of the post-war boom in the whisky industry, partly set in Glasgow.

284 RAE, HUGH C. *Night pillow*. Anthony Blond, 1967.
Develops after a rather sensational opening into a well-plotted, dramatic but credible story, drawing together the lives of a hastily married teenage couple and a group of tough boys. Particularly notable for its closely observed background of cheerless, vast housing schemes contrasting with cosy suburbia, and for a nightmarish final chase sequence in a block of high flats. Three of Rae's other novels, *Skinner* (1965), *A few small bones* (1968), and *The Saturday epic* (1970), have Glasgow scenes, though essentially set in neighbouring counties.

285 SHARP, ALAN. *A green tree in Gedde*. Michael Joseph, 1965.
Only partly set in Glasgow and to a greater extent in Greenock, but the treatment of both has an unusual poetic realism, capturing scene and atmosphere with great clarity and sympathy. The sequel, *The wind shifts* (1967), is not set in Glasgow.

286 SPENCE, ALAN. *Its colours they are fine*. Collins, 1977.
An extremely fine story sequence, building through linked but separate stories into a sharp, precisely observed delineation of Glasgow life from childhood on. Particularly telling are the early stories which, almost casually, trace the degeneration of a streetwise urchin into a 'hard man'.

287 TORRINGTON, JEFF. *Swing hammer swing!* Secker and Warburg, 1992.

A weekend in the life of Thomas Clay during the late 1960s as he waits for the birth of his first child and the demolition, along with the rest of the Gorbals, of his tenement home. The surreal atmosphere of the time is captured with black humour, alongside great bitterness at the destruction of a community. Whitbread Book of the Year 1993.

288 TROCCHI, ALEXANDER. *Young Adam.* Paris: Olympia Press, 1954.

Originally published under the pseudonym Frances Lengel; first British publication 1961. Joe helps to recover the body of a drowned woman from the Forth and Clyde Canal, knowing more about her death than he reveals at first to the reader; the knowledge adds tension to his subsequent sexual encounters, and drives him to spectate at the trial in Glasgow of a man suspected of the murder.

289 TROCCHI, ALEXANDER. *Cain's book.* New York: Grove, 1960.

First British publication 1963. Joe Necchi, aboard a scow off New York, is injecting heroin and writing *Cain's Book*; the grim depiction of his present lifestyle is backed by memories, sharp and often humorous, of a Glasgow childhood.

290 WILKINSON, RODERICK. *Murder belongs to me!* Museum Press, 1956.

Thriller set in contemporary Glasgow; a private eye becomes involved with a super-gang running organised crime in the city under the guise of Scottish Republican action.

291 WODEN, GEORGE [pseud. of G. W. Slaney]. *Simonetta.* Hutchinson, 1952.

Contemporary novel, partly set in Glasgow (see annotation to 205-209). In his *The puzzled policeman* (1949), children help to solve a mystery in the Queen's Park area.

292 YOUNG, ARTHUR, *pseud. The surgeon's apprentice.* Glasgow: LindsayPublications, 1997.

A prequel to *The surgeon's knot* (413), though longer and more diffuse, and hence rather less effective; follows Neil Aitken through his medical training in the late 1940s, with associated problems of life and love.

X 1970-

293 BANKS, IAIN. *Espedair Street.* Macmillan, 1987.

Barricaded from the world in a mad mock church in St Vincent Street (not the Greek Thomson masterpiece), Danny Weir, millionaire rock musician now retired at thirty-one, reflects on a career which took him from a housing scheme in Paisley to disaster in Miami. A rock novel which, as a bonus, depicts Glasgow in the run-up to its Year of Culture: 'Fresh paint on the double yellow lines an a bigger subsidy fur the opera'.

294 BANKS, IAIN. *The crow road.* Scribners, 1992.

Humour and tragedy together as the young narrator unravels the long-ago mystery of his Uncle Rory's disappearance. The novel moves freely among at least three time-zones and as many viewpoints, presenting a complex family story. The setting is mainly a fictionalised Argyll, but extended sequences in the west end of Glasgow culminate in a surreally splendid Park Circus flat.

295 BARCLAY, JAMES. *The bigot*. Greenock: Seannachaidh Publishing, 1989.

Novelisation of a popular 'seventies play, treating sectarianism in Glasgow in terms of broad comedy. *Still a bigot* (Glasgow: Lindsay Publications, 1997) is a sequel.

296 BERMANT, CHAIM. *The second Mrs Whitberg*. Allen and Unwin, 1976.

Rich, funny Jewish-background novel documenting the search for the second Mrs Whitberg (not particularly desired by the widowed Mr Whitberg, but felt essential by his well-wishers) and also the shifting pattern of Glasgow society as Jewish residents, once themselves newcomers, reluctantly move out of their terrace before the incoming Pakistani families.

297 BOYCE, CHRIS. *Blooding Mr Naylor*. Glasgow: Dog and Bone, 1990.

In the 'new Glasgow' of the late 'eighties, an old woman famous as a left-wing nationalist is found battered to death, and lawyer Jack Naylor is called in to represent a peace camper accused of the murder. An edgy, violent political thriller follows from the complicated allegiances of the victim, the accused and Naylor himself.

298 BOYD, EDWARD *and* KNOX, BILL. *The view from Daniel Pike*. Arrow Books, 1974.

From a TV series; episodes in the career of a tough Glasgow private investigator with his own reluctant integrity.

299 BOYD, EDWARD *and* PARKES, ROGER. *The dark number*. Constable, 1973.

A Glasgow thriller, accurate in setting: a man's search for his missing wife reopens old wounds and the mystery of his daughter's drowning.

300 BROOKMYRE, CHRISTOPHER. *Country of the blind*. Little, Brown, 1997.

A superior thriller, set largely in Edinburgh and the Highlands, but opening with an extended Glasgow sequence as a young woman lawyer, struggling to acclimatise to the city and its people, is drawn into a plot of murder and conspiracy.

301 BURGESS, MOIRA *and* WHYTE, HAMISH *eds. Streets of gold: contemporary Glasgow stories*. Edinburgh: Mainstream, 1989.

Twenty-four short stories set in Glasgow or by Glasgow writers, all written during the period 1979-88.

302 BURKE, RAYMOND. *Spoutmouth*. Glasgow: dualchas, 1995.

An unemployed young man in the depths of depression begins to keep a diary; between the lines we discover that he has lost touch with reality, and that, in passing, he is killing almost at random. A powerful comment on 1990s life.

303 CAMPSIE, ALISTAIR. *By law protected*. Edinburgh: Canongate, 1976.

Only partly set in Glasgow, but includes a nightmarish street scene on the day of a Rangers-Celtic cup final; also a blackly humorous account of the forming of a suicide brigade from the Glasgow slums, organised on sectarian lines.

304 CANNON, MICHAEL. *The borough*. Serpent's Tail, 1995.

Partick in the closing days of the twentieth century, where a group of characters is observed by an unnamed narrator from another dimension; a slightly uneasy blend of realism and millennial fever.

305 CATHCART, ALEX. *The comeback.* Edinburgh: Polygon, 1986.
Opens in 1960s Glasgow when Hamish Creese, having fallen foul of the debt-collector Gaffney, is nailed to the floor in a dockside pub. After years overseas he returns to find Glasgow much changed and Gaffney an acclaimed poet, unmindful of the violence which changed Hamish's life.

306 CATHCART, ALEX. *The missionary.* Edinburgh: Polygon, 1988.
Dave Parks, newly-qualified social worker, has problems with the retired African missionary who has been assigned to him for help, but a deeper personal problem as, isolated from the working class in which he grew up, he adjusts to his own changed status.

307 CAVE, PETER. *Taggart: murder in season.* Glasgow: Scottish Television *and* Edinburgh: Mainstream Publishing, 1985.

308 CAVE, PETER. *Gingerbread.* Edinburgh: Mainstream 1993.

309 CAVE, PETER. *Nest of vipers.* Edinburgh: Mainstream, 1993.

310 CAVE, PETER. *Fatal inheritance.* Edinburgh: Mainstream, 1994.

311 CAVE, PETER. *Forbidden fruit.* Edinburgh: Mainstream, 1994.
Novelisations of *Taggart* stories (see 312), Glenn Chandler being credited as scriptwriter in each case.

312 CHANDLER, GLENN. *Killer.* Glasgow: Scottish Television *and* Edinburgh: Mainstream Publishing, 1983.
Police procedural in which a disillusioned Glasgow policeman and his young assistant investigate a series of murders in the city. Based on the first episode of the long-running and immensely popular STV series *Taggart*; transfers awkwardly to print.

313 CLOSE, AJAY. *Official and doubtful.* Secker and Warburg, 1996.
Nan, employed in the Returned Letters department of the GPO in central Glasgow, finds an insufficiently addressed blackmail note and sets out on a somewhat implausible personal quest to trace the addressee. She becomes closely involved with the three possible candidates, and the secret in her own past is eventually revealed.

314 COLE, GERALD. *Comfort and joy.* Methuen, 1984.
Based on the screenplay by Bill Forsyth for his film about a Glasgow ice-cream war, hence visual rather than literary: a light, mildly comic tale, with little hint of the escalation which overtook the ice-cream wars story in real life.

315 COWAN, EVELYN. *Portrait of Alice.* Edinburgh: Canongate, 1976.
The powerful story of a fifty-year-old woman coming home after a nervous breakdown into much the same conditions which triggered it. The death of her son, her husband's impotence (and infidelity), the pressure of Jewish suburban society, build up on Alice as she grimly tries to reconstruct her life by her own resources.

316 CRAIG, BILL *and* MILLER, HUGH. *The mourning brooch.* New English Library, 1978.

Thriller set in contemporary Glasgow: a shady property developer hunts for the missing heir whose signature can save him from disaster.

317 DAVIS, MARGARET THOMSON. *The prisoner.* Allison and Busby, 1974.
Credible conflict of class and religion as a frustrated Bearsden housewife, prisoner of her upbringing and environment, sees her teenage daughter unworriedly involved with a working-class Catholic boy from Maryhill.

318 DAVIS, MARGARET THOMSON. *A very civilised man.* Allison and Busby, 1982.
A restless, depressed wife slips into an affair with a charming and selfish university lecturer, but finds the maturity to break free and begin a new life on her own.

319 DAVIS, MARGARET THOMSON. *A kind of immortality.* Century, 1996.
Set in the 1980s; a sequel to *Hold me forever* (239) and *Kiss me no more* (240) in taking up the story of Andrina's daughter Jennifer who runs away to London, but centres on a new character, forty-year-old Bessie, who leaves her unhappy marriage to exercise her gift for painting.

320 DEELEY, NORMAN. *Jargon Hall.* Braunton: Merlin Books, 1984.
Lively satire on teacher-training and school conditions in Glasgow.

321 DICKSON, JACK. *Oddfellows.* Brighton: Millivres Books, 1997.
Outspoken exploration of 'the gay underworld of Glasgow'.

322 DOLAN, CHRIS. *Poor angels, and other stories.* Edinburgh: Polygon, 1995.
Sixteen short stories, most set in Glasgow. Strange goings-on with a stone angel in the title story; a beautifully unsentimental look at old age in the prizewinning 'Sleet and snow'.

323 GALLOWAY, JANICE. *Blood.* Secker and Warburg, 1991.
Glasgow provides a setting for several of these short stories, shot with black humour, violence and surrealism.

324 GRAHAM, BARRY. *Of darkness and light.* Bloomsbury, 1989.
Bizarre horror story, perhaps over the top in its depiction of a very gory Glasgow.

325 GRAHAM, BARRY. *The champion's new clothes.* Bloomsbury, 1991.
The action moves between Edinburgh and Glasgow in the preparation for a world title fight; a journalist and ex-boxer joins the challenger's retinue, finding this to some extent a welcome diversion from his disturbed love-life.

326 GRAHAM, BARRY. *Get out as early as you can.* Bloomsbury, 1992.
Grim short stories, several set in Glasgow, exploring a bleak, violent urban world.

327 GRAHAM, BARRY. *The book of man.* Serpent's Tail, 1995.
A playwright/performance artist returns to Glasgow after ten years' absence, looking for the truth about a friend's death but finding also his own past. In part a waspish *roman à clef* of the contemporary Glasgow literary scene.

328 GRAY, ALASDAIR. *Lanark.* Edinburgh: Canongate, 1981.
It is tempting, though probably wrong, to see *Lanark* as two novels distinct in style but unified by a shifting pattern of reference and allusion. The substantially realistic life-story of Duncan Thaw, Glasgow art student in the 1950s, is surrounded

and as it were exploded by the first and last sections, in which Lanark, a dreamlike approximation to Thaw, moves through a surreal world where a nightmare future Glasgow may be glimpsed or imagined. The novel was at once recognised as unique in Glasgow fiction for its originality and breadth of vision. Much has been written about *Lanark* and its influence, but in any interpretation its publication was a landmark in Glasgow (and Scottish) fiction.

329 GRAY, ALASDAIR. *Unlikely stories, mostly.* Edinburgh: Canongate, 1983.
Glasgow appears from time to time, by name or recognisable allusion, in these notably individual short stories.

330 GRAY, ALASDAIR. *1982, Janine.* Jonathan Cape, 1984.
Brilliantly conceived treatment of the serial fantasy in the mind of a lonely, ageing alcoholic, set within the real story of his boyhood and unhappy marriage, with haunting echoes and shifts from one to the other. The novel is in part a homage to MacDiarmid's poem *A drunk man looks at the thistle*, and 'the matter of Scotland' is an important theme.

331 GRAY, ALASDAIR. *Something leather.* Jonathan Cape, 1990.
The result of Gray's decision to essay a novel from a woman's point of view, though the viewpoint is a lesbian sado-masochistic one, perhaps a shade atypical. The main story is intercut with loosely connected episodes, in part revisions of earlier work.

332 GRAY, ALASDAIR. *Ten tales tall and true.* Bloomsbury, 1993.
Fourteen, actually (Gray remarks on the discrepancy in a title-page verse); several of these stories and prose pieces are set in contemporary Glasgow, others (such as 'Near the driver') in much more disturbing times and places.

333 GRAY, ALASDAIR. *Mavis Belfrage: a romantic novel; with five shorter tales.* Bloomsbury, 1996.
The title novella is set in Edinburgh, but four of the other pieces reflect aspects of Gray's Glasgow: all deal with 'folk in Britain's lowest professional class', namely teachers.

334 HAMILTON, ALEX. *Gallus, did you say? and other stories.* Glasgow: Ferret Press, 1982.
Seven authentic, bleakly amusing short stories, mostly reflecting childhood and adolescence in Glasgow housing schemes, written in phoneticised Glasgow dialect: 'representing ... the first conscious decision to reproduce in extended written prose the sounds of Glasgow English'.

335 HAMILTON, ALEX *and others. Three Glasgow writers.* Glasgow: Molendinar Press, 1976.
Short stories by Hamilton and James Kelman; also the story 'Honest' and several poems by Tom Leonard.

336 HILDREY, MIKE. *Sharks.* Glendaruel: Argyll Publishing, 1996.
Unsparing indictment of the loan-shark culture in contemporary post-Thatcher Glasgow.

337 HODGMAN, JACKIE. *The fish in white sauce incident.* Aberdeen: Keith Murray Publishing, 1992.
   Ten powerful short stories, most set in Glasgow.

338 HURD, DOUGLAS *and* OSMOND, ANDREW. *Scotch on the rocks.* Collins, 1971.
   Political thriller suggesting sinister developments in Scottish nationalism; set some ten years after publication date. Though the action is mainly in the Highlands, the book opens with an extended sequence set in Glasgow: gangs v. police in Blackhill, and charismatic political speechmaking on Glasgow Green.

339 JAMIESON, SANDY. *Own goal.* Glasgow: Ringwood Publishing, 1997.
   Set in 1990: a man on a revenge mission which culminates in a plan to assassinate Mrs Thatcher at a Hampden cup final. The central character's obsessions are football, politics and sex, not necessarily in that order.

340 JENKINS, ROBIN. *Willie Hogg.* Edinburgh: Polygon, 1993.
   Willie and his wife Maggie are flown to Arizona, where Maggie's sister is dying, by a tabloid newspaper tapping into the legendary Glaswegian warmth and generosity; but Jenkins probes motives and relationships in a complex novel.

341 JOHNSTON, ANDREW. *Cuckoo plot.* Dumfries: Criffel Books, 1996.
   Thriller about Irish terrorist operations in 1970s Glasgow.

342 KELMAN, JAMES. *An old pub near the Angel, and other stories.* Orono, Maine: Puckerbush Press, 1973.
   Thirteen short stories, mainly set in Glasgow. Kelman's first short story collection; 'The cards' possibly foreshadows his first novel *The busconductor Hines* (345).

343 KELMAN, JAMES. *Short tales from the night shift.* Glasgow: Print Studio Press, 1978.
   Very short stories, including the classic 'Acid'. Several have not so far appeared in later collections.

344 KELMAN, JAMES. *Not not while the giro, and other stories.* Edinburgh: Polygon Books, 1983.
   Twenty-six short stories mainly set in Glasgow; only two appear in his earlier collection *An old pub near the angel* (342).

345 KELMAN, JAMES. *The busconductor Hines.* Edinburgh: Polygon Books, 1984.
   A notable first novel tracing the crumbling of a man's world at work and at home. Hines is likeable as well as believable; his relations with his wife and son are delicately handled, and he is seen at the end to be maintaining a precarious balance among the potentially crushing pressures of his life.

346 KELMAN, JAMES. *A chancer.* Edinburgh: Polygon Books, 1985.
   Examination of a compulsive gambler, in whose life betting takes priority over family, friends and work. Tammas is perhaps a less attractive and fully realised character than Hines (see 345), but Kelman's depiction of Glasgow life is unremittingly authentic.

347 KELMAN, JAMES. *Greyhound for breakfast.* Secker and Warburg, 1987.
   Forty-seven short stories written 1972-87, many set in Glasgow, continuing

Kelman's exploration of a bleak world previously unacknowledged in fiction.

348 KELMAN, JAMES. *A disaffection*. Secker and Warburg, 1989.
'Patrick Doyle was a teacher. Gradually he had become sickened by it', and this novel follows him through one week in his life, during which problems of work, family and love drive him to something near despair.

349 KELMAN, JAMES. *The burn*. Secker and Warburg, 1991.
Twenty-six short stories, most set in Glasgow, reaching at times (as in 'By the burn') an extraordinary level of concentrated emotion.

350 KELMAN, JAMES. *How late it was, how late*. Secker and Warburg, 1994.
A brilliant novel told entirely from the viewpoint of a man who wakes in police custody to find he is blind. The DSS suspiciously classes his condition as Sightloss; he tries to survive in a dark world. Awarded the Booker Prize in 1994.

351 KELMAN, JAMES *ed. An East End anthology 1988*. Glasgow: Clydeside Press, 1988.
Several fine short stories with Glasgow settings appear in this collection of work from a writers' group which Kelman assisted for two years.

352 KELMAN, JAMES *and others. Lean tales*. Jonathan Cape, 1985.
Short stories by Kelman, Agnes Owens and Alasdair Gray. Not all are set in Glasgow, but they speak with a Glasgow voice and are concerned with the industrial West of Scotland.

353 KENNEDY, A. L. *Night geometry and the Garscadden trains*. Edinburgh: Polygon, 1991.
Fifteen brilliant short stories, most set in Glasgow.

354 KENNEDY, A. L. *Looking for the possible dance*. Secker and Warburg, 1993.
A train journey from Glasgow to London gives Margaret time and space to think about her single-parent father, her on-and-off lover, the sad harassing boss who has just fired her; the memories interpenetrate her encounter with a disabled young man on the train to make a compelling network of past and present, held in the structure of the journey.

355 KENNEDY, A. L. *So I am glad*. Jonathan Cape, 1995.
Magical realism in contemporary Glasgow. Jennifer, damaged by childhood abuse and alternating between frigidity and violent sado-masochistic sessions, encounters the healing influence of an inexplicable visitor, the seventeenth-century Frenchman Cyrano de Bergerac.

356 KENNEDY, A. L. *Original bliss*. Jonathan Cape, 1997.
In the title novella of this volume (which also includes ten short stories with various settings) Helen Brindle, stranded in contemporary middle-class Glasgow with her violent husband, escapes to join a psychology professor whose theories fascinate her. He proves to have an obsession with pornography: the situation which develops is delicately and strongly explored.

357 LEEMING, BRUCE. *Now you must dance*. Edinburgh: Scottish Cultural Press, 1996.
Political novel in favour of Scottish independence, set in Glasgow in 1995.

358 LINDSAY, FREDERIC. *Brond*. Edinburgh: Macdonald Publishers, 1984.

An impressive first novel, gripping as a political thriller but with disturbing depths and echoes to be found behind the story. A surreal suggestion of evil possibilities underlies the clearly-realised Glasgow scene as the narrator becomes involved with the mysterious, near-omnipotent Brond.

359 LINDSAY, FREDERIC. *Jill rips.* Andre Deutsch, 1987.
In an unnamed city recognisable as Glasgow, a policeman is drawn more intimately than he wants into the search for a serial killer; the dates match those of Jack the Ripper's killings in Victorian London, but the victims are men and the letter claiming to be from the killer is signed 'Jill'.

360 McALLISTER, ANGUS. *The Krugg syndrome.* Grafton, 1988.
A comedy science-fiction novel set in Glasgow.

361 McBAIN, HUGH. *The brothers Gordian: public investigators.* Glasgow: Jordanbooks, 1993.
Heavily humorous crime story involving the eponymous brothers, private eyes in 1990s Glasgow.

362 McBAIN, HUGH. *Man's book.* Glasgow: Jordanbooks, 1996.
An ambitious attempt to view 'the human story as it approaches the end of the second millennium AD'; some episodes set in Glasgow.

363 McCABE, MARY. *Everwinding times.* Glendaruel: Argyll Publishing, 1994.
Rooted in contemporary Glasgow but ranges from the 1950s to the early 21st century, since the central character Ailie has a strange condition which causes her to wake from sleep into different periods of time; the device is used as a means of considering the course of one woman's life.

364 McDERMID, VAL. *Final edition.* The Women's Press, 1991.
The spruced-up Glasgow of 1990 supplies local colour as lesbian reporter/ investigator Lindsay Gordon seeks the murderer of an ex-lover. Other novels in this series are not set in Glasgow.

365 MacDOUGALL, CARL. *Prosepiece.* Markinch: Pavement Press, 1979.
Six short stories or vignettes, several with Glasgow settings, of which only two are reprinted in *Elvis is dead* (367).

366 MacDOUGALL, CARL. *The one legged tap dancer.* Glasgow: Print Studio Press, 1981.
Long short story: episodes, with vivid cameos, in a student's progress through a range of jobs including mortuary porter, dishwasher, encyclopedia salesman, and GPO casual worker.

367 MacDOUGALL, CARL. *Elvis is dead.* Glasgow: Mariscat Press, 1986.
Nineteen short stories, mostly set in contemporary Glasgow.

368 MacDOUGALL, CARL. *Stone over water.* Secker and Warburg, 1989.
Angus MacPhail, middle-aged bank manager, writes two interleaved narratives, moving between the golden 'sixties and the disenchanted 'eighties to build up a picture of his unsatisfactory life.

369 MacDOUGALL, CARL. *The lights below.* Secker and Warburg, 1993.

Released from jail, Andy sets out to find the person who framed him, but equally to come to terms with how prison has changed him. Glasgow too has changed, and that story runs alongside Andy's in passages of lyrical bitterness.

370 MacDOUGALL, CARL. *The Casanova papers.* Secker and Warburg, 1996.
A recently widowed man writes to his children, reconstructing his married life for them and for himself; he finds resonances in contemporary accounts of Casanova which expand and illuminate Casanova's own autobiographical version.

371 McGINNESS, IAIN. *Inner city.* Edinburgh: Polygon, 1987.
Grim portrayal of contemporary Glasgow through the stories of car worker Pat, teacher Sam and bigamist Alec. Interpolated commentaries on Glasgow history, customs and sectarianism add their deeply pessimistic points.

372 McILVANNEY, WILLIAM. *Laidlaw.* Hodder and Stoughton, 1977.
Outstanding police thriller in which loner Detective-Inspector Laidlaw moves through an authentically and sensitively portrayed Glasgow; not just a detective story but a classic Glasgow novel. See 373 and 374 for further exploration of Laidlaw, and note the appearance of characters from all three books in other novels by McIlvanney not primarily set in Glasgow, building up a unified fictional world.

373 McILVANNEY, WILLIAM. *The papers of Tony Veitch.* Hodder and Stoughton, 1983.
A sequel to *Laidlaw* (372) and even less of a police-procedural thriller; a student's disappearance ties into the Glasgow underworld of hard men, violence, grudges and revenge.

374 McILVANNEY, WILLIAM. *Strange loyalties.* Hodder and Stoughton, 1991.
Jack Laidlaw (see 372 and 373) tries to make sense of his brother's apparently meaningless death; told in the first person, taking us further into the character of the complex, unconventional Laidlaw.

375 McKAY, RON. *The prophet.* New English Library, 1992.
Serial killings in Glasgow with suspicion falling on an embittered ex-pop star, who makes it his business to track down the murderer.

376 McKAY, RON. *Mean city.* Hodder and Stoughton, 1995.
Begins as a sequel to *No mean city* (185), carrying forward the story of Razor King's brother Peter Stark; continues into the 1990s as Peter's son (Johnnie, named after his famous uncle) becomes a leading figure on the contemporary Glasgow crime scene.

377 McKAY, RON. *The leper colony.* Victor Gollancz, 1997.
An intriguing start as the central character discovers, on the death of his father, that he has been living since childhood under an assumed name. He returns to Glasgow to investigate, with a slight decrease in plausibility as MI6 recruits him to clean up the city's drugs scene.

378 McLAUGHLIN, BRENDAN *ed. A spiel amang us: Glasgow people writing.* Edinburgh: Mainstream, 1990.
Anthology of short stories, poems and non-fiction pieces submitted for the Scotia

Bar Writers' Prize, on the general theme 'The Art and Politics of Living in Scotland'. Several stories set in Glasgow.

379 MacLAVERTY, BERNARD. *Grace notes.* Jonathan Cape, 1997.

Catherine's journey home to Northern Ireland for her father's funeral is the introduction to earlier events in Islay and Glasgow: the birth of her child, post-natal depression, and the first broadcast of a musical composition which (like the novel) finds an epiphany through the remembered threat of the Lambeg drums.

380 McLAY, FARQUHAR *ed. Workers city.* Glasgow: Clydeside Press, 1988.

Collection of short stories, poetry and non-fiction pieces setting forth 'the real Glasgow' ahead of the Year of Culture 1990, which was strenuously opposed by the organisation Workers City. A subsequent collection *The reckoning* (1990) reviews the year from the same viewpoint, but contains no fiction.

381 MacLEOD, KEN. *The stone canal.* Legend, 1996.

Science-fiction novel set mainly in the mid-21st century and on a distant planet, but chapters 2 and 4 take place in 1975 Glasgow.

382 MAIR, ALISTAIR. *The Douglas affair.* Heinemann, 1966.

Set 'somewhere in the future': a wealthy Glasgow businessman's organisation of a new Scottish nationalist party. Not of high literary quality, but ingenious, if over-dramatic, in its working out of the situation.

383 MAY, PETER. *The reporter.* Corgi Books, 1978.

A hard-bitten reporter on a Glasgow daily paper investigates possible international sabotage on a North Sea oil-rig. Based on a short-lived TV series, *The Standard.*

384 MILLER, HUGH. *The open city.* New English Library, 1973.

'Novel of the Glasgow underworld', though it is a cosmopolitan underworld that might be set in any city. Seedy small-time crook Alec McBain rings most true: having been in prison during the reorganisation of Glasgow's traffic flow, he is killed crossing an unexpected one-way street.

385 MILLS, JOSEPH. *Towards the end.* Edinburgh: Polygon, 1989.

The first openly gay Glasgow novel: a young man's search for a meaningful relationship.

386 MOONEY, MARY [pseud. of John Rodger]. *Sfalick (Deirdre's lament).* Glasgow: dualchas, 1994.

Surreal, funny and desperate monologue of a young woman trapped in a DSS-supplied flat with her wheelchair-bound mother whom she has abducted from a home: the design of the book, with a hole punched through covers and pages, confirms that there is no centre to Deirdre's life.

387 MORIN, CAROLE. *Dead glamorous.* Gollancz, 1996.

An autobiographical novel, or fictionalised autobiography, which progresses at great speed through the narrator's Hollywood-obsessed life, from complicated family affairs in the east end of Glasgow to London and beyond.

388 MORTON, TOM. *Red guitars in heaven.* Edinburgh: Mainstream, 1994.

An odyssey, with guitar, from an evangelical Ayrshire childhood to bohemian West End Glasgow and second-hand bookselling in the Highlands; includes *The rats of fear* (the title is from a Trocchi poem), the ultimate Glasgow detective novel, which unfortunately consists of only Chapter One.

389 O'GAFFERTY, F. N. *Helsinki (not the town)*. Glasgow: dualchas, 1995.

Sixteen short pieces with Glasgow relevance, several marked by startling black humour.

390 OLIPHANT, WILLIAM. *A therapy of camels*. Edinburgh: Chapman, 1995.

The settings of these short stories range widely in place and time, but several are grounded in contemporary Glasgow.

391 PAIGE, FRANCES [pseud. of May W. Martin]. *Kindred spirits*. Harper Collins, 1997.

Sequel to *The Glasgow girls* (195), *The painted ladies* (277) and *The butterfly girl* (278), concluding the stories of Anna and Jean Mackintosh; set in Glasgow and USA during the early 1970s.

392 PALLISER, CHARLES. *The sensationist*. Jonathan Cape, 1991.

The protagonist, in a stressful short-term job in the financial sector, moves from bed to bed through an unnamed but clearly realised 'eighties Glasgow, intending to remain detached. His involvement leads to violence: 'What I did was harmless enough... It wasn't to be expected that I should foresee everything'.

393 PALLISER, CHARLES. *Betrayals*. Jonathan Cape, 1994.

A mystery story involving, *inter alia*, plagiarism and serial killing, in which each of the ten chapters is a pastiche of a literary genre, writer or work (including a TV crime series called *Biggert*; see 307-312). The setting is contemporary Glasgow and the dedication hints at a *roman à clef*.

394 RAE, HUGH C. *The marksman*. Constable, 1971.

A hard-edged thriller: the central character returns to Glasgow after five years on the London crime scene to investigate and avenge the murder of his twelve-year-old son.

395 RANKIN, IAN. *Black and blue*. Orion, 1997.

The memory of Bible John, real-life Glasgow serial killer of the 1960s, is revived by murders in several Scottish cities, and the copycat killer is pursued not only by police but by the real Bible John. Awarded the Gold Dagger of the Crime Writers' Association in 1997.

396 REILLY, HUGH. *Kelly!* Glasgow: Embros Publications, 1996.

Leaden humour in a teenager's quest for self-discovery as a rookie policeman in the east end of Glasgow.

397 RODGER, JOHN. *3*. Glasgow: dualchas, 1993.

Three short pieces, experimental and surreal in style, set in contemporary Glasgow.

398 SCOTT, MANDA. *Hen's teeth*. Women's Press, 1996.

Medical training and cat-burglary skills are equally useful to a lively lesbian investigator and her friend seeking the truth behind the death of an ex-lover; a fast-moving thriller set partly in the west end of Glasgow.

399 SMITH, IAIN CRICHTON. *Goodbye, Mr Dixon*. Gollancz, 1974.

A deceptively quiet beginning, set in an unnamed but recognisable Glasgow, builds to explosive excitement as the hero explores his past and uncovers a forgotten trauma.

400 SMITH, IAIN CRICHTON. *A field full of folk*. Gollancz, 1982.

A fine novel of contemporary Highland life, in which two brief but important chapters depict Glasgow as a place first to escape to, then to escape from.

401 SMITH, IAIN CRICHTON. *The dream*. Macmillan, 1990.

Essentially an examination of the contemporary state of Gaeldom and the Gaelic language, explored through the relationship of an island-born couple long resident in Glasgow. Sharp picture of the city from a Hebridean perspective.

402 SMITH, MARK. *Masel*. Taranis Books, 1992.

Slightly unreal adventures of an American folk-music expert in Glasgow during the Year of Culture 1990.

403 SPENCE, ALAN. *The magic flute*. Edinburgh: Canongate, 1990.

Spans the 'sixties and 'seventies; follows the lives of four Govan boys – the clever one, the musician, the dullard and the tearaway – from the point where, as twelve-year-olds, they turn up for flute lessons from the local bandmaster.

404 SPENCE, ALAN. *Stone garden, and other stories*. Phoenix House, 1995.

Twelve short stories set in Glasgow or with Glasgow reference; some remember a 1960s childhood, but the ambience is contemporary and the present day thoughtfully considered.

405 SUTHERLAND, DOUGLAS. *Strike!* Heinemann, 1976.

Set in contemporary Clydebank.

406 SWEET, PAT. *Troubled waters*. Virago, 1994.

Cat O'Connell, feisty Glasgow-based female private investigator in the V.I. Warshawski tradition, looks into a series of 'accidents' in the oil industry and her lover's mysterious death.

407 TAYLOR, JIM. *Wasters*. Milngavie: Lipstick and Lager Publications, 1983.

Eight short stories, reflecting the effects of the recession in contemporary Glasgow, which clumsily but sincerely reproduce the passions and pains of unemployed youth.

408 TURNBULL, PETER. *Deep and crisp and even*. Collins, 1981.

A good police thriller conveying the atmosphere of snow-covered Glasgow gripped in terror during a series of psychopathic murders. The headquarters of P Division is notionally at Charing Cross and its saga is continued in *Dead knock* (1982), *Fair Friday* (1983), *Big money* (1984), *Two way cut* (1988), *Condition purple* (1989), *And did murder him* (1991), *Long day Monday* (1992), and *The killing floor* (1994). The police characters, broadly drawn, do not develop greatly over the series, but we may note the obligatory bent cop in *Big money* and a sympathetic look at

Glasgow prostitutes in *Condition purple*.

409 TURNBULL, PETER. *The justice game: the lady from Rome.* BBC Books, 1990.
   Novelisation of a TV series featuring a Glasgow lawyer.

410 VALLANCE, DOUGLAS. *The Milngavie connection.* Hale, 1977.
   A Glasgow University lecturer witnesses a murder; a manhunt through Glasgow
   and Milngavie to the West Highlands ensues.

411 WHYTE, CHRISTOPHER. *Euphemia McFarrigle and the laughing virgin.* Gollancz,
   1995.
   Broad humour co-exists with tragedy and magical realism in this unique novel,
   which, under the fun, contains an unsparing critique of the Catholic church's attitude
   to homosexuality.

412 WOOD, JAMES. *North beat.* Hutchinson, 1973.
   Police procedural set in 'a large Scottish city' probably recognisable as Glasgow.
   His earlier and slighter thriller *The shop in Loch Street* (1958) has a more definite
   Glasgow setting.

413 YOUNG, ARTHUR, *pseud. The surgeon's knot.* Collins, 1982.
   Impressive first novel of a young, overworked Glasgow hospital doctor, about to
   leave for America, who questions his decision as he treats ailments that he
   recognises as 'cries for help'. See prequel *The surgeon's apprentice* (292).

Chronological Index of Novels
by year of first publication

Author Index

SPENCE, ALAN (1947-)

STEWART, ALFRED WALTER (1880-1947) *see* CONNINGTON, J. J. *pseud.*

STIRLING, JESSICA [pseud. of Hugh C. Rae, *q.v.*]

STRAIN, EUPHANS H. (-1934)

SUTHERLAND, DOUGLAS

SWAN, ANNIE SHEPHERD [*i.e. Mrs* James Burnett Smith]

SWEET, PAT

TAIT, W. CUMMING

TAYLOR, CHARLES (c. 1795-1837)

TAYLOR, ELIZABETH

TAYLOR, JIM (1963-)

TEADDY, *pseud.*

TORRINGTON, JEFF (1935-)

TROCCHI, ALEXANDER (1925-84)

TURNBULL, PETER (1950-)

Title Index

135